W9-BDV-590

BONES NEVER LIE

How Forensics Helps Solve History's Mysteries

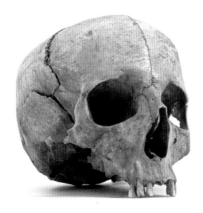

Elizabeth MacLeod

annick press
toronto + new york + vancouver

© 2013 Elizabeth MacLeod (text)
Edited by Kathy Lowinger
Designed by Sheryl Shapiro
Second printing, June 2013

Annick Press Ltd.

We acknowledge the support of the Canada Council for the Arts, the Ontario Arts Council, and the Government of Canada through the Canada Book Fund (CBF) for our publishing activities.

ONTARIO ARTS COUNCIL
CONSEIL DES ARTS DE L'ONTARIO

Cataloging in Publication
MacLeod, Elizabeth
    Bones never lie : how forensics helps solve history's
mysteries / Elizabeth MacLeod.

Includes bibliographical references and index.
Issued also in electronic formats.
ISBN 978-1-55451-483-0 (bound).—ISBN 978-1-55451-482-3 (pbk.)

    1. Forensic anthropology—Juvenile literature. 2. Forensic
sciences—Juvenile literature. I. Title.

GN69.8.M33 2013   j614'.17   C2012-905702-9

Distributed in Canada by:
Firefly Books Ltd.
50 Staples Avenue, Unit 1
Richmond Hill, ON L4B 0A7

Published in the U.S.A. by Annick Press (U.S.) Ltd.
Distributed in the U.S.A. by:
Firefly Books (U.S.) Inc.
P.O. Box 1338
Ellicott Station
Buffalo, NY 14205

Printed in China

Also available in e-book format. Please visit
www.annickpress.com/ebooks for more details. Or scan

With much love and admiration for
Frieda, a great author and friend
E.M.

Visit us at: www.annickpress.com

Contents

Acknowledgments

Thanks to the many people who worked their fingers to the bone to help me with this book. Special thanks to editor Kathy Lowinger, and to managing editors Chandra Wohleber and Katie Hearn. Thanks always to Brigitte Waisberg.

No bones about it—it was such a pleasure to work again with the fantastic photo researcher Sandra Booth and the incredible designer Sheryl Shapiro. I'm so grateful for everything they did to make this book look terrific. Also much appreciated is the very careful work of copy editor Catherine Dorton and proofreaders Claudia Kutchukian, Liba Berry, and Joanna Karaplis.

Thank you to Dad, John, and Douglas. Love and thanks to Paul for his help and support—and that's no lie!

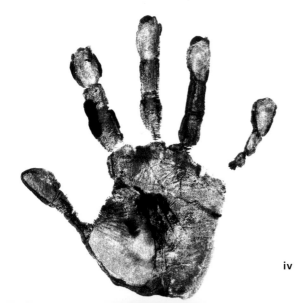

Forensics: The Key to History's Mysteries

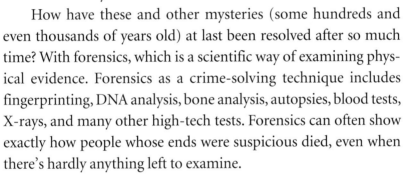

Some of history's most intriguing mysteries have finally been solved!

How did King Tut die?

Was Napoleon poisoned?

Did Princess Anastasia escape the terrible fate suffered by the rest of her family?

How have these and other mysteries (some hundreds and even thousands of years old) at last been resolved after so much time? With forensics, which is a scientific way of examining physical evidence. Forensics as a crime-solving technique includes fingerprinting, DNA analysis, bone analysis, autopsies, blood tests, X-rays, and many other high-tech tests. Forensics can often show exactly how people whose ends were suspicious died, even when there's hardly anything left to examine.

People love a mystery, and when it involves royalty and all the power, money, and prestige that go with it, the stakes are raised and the story becomes irresistible. You might think there wouldn't be much mystery about people as famous and powerful as monarchs and their families; isn't everything they do public and well documented?

But paparazzi, security cameras, and investigative reporting are modern developments. The written accounts that were the main source of information in the past were sometimes recorded inaccurately in the first place, changed, or misinterpreted. And many records have gone missing over the years, either accidentally or deliberately.

Mysteries surrounding royals stay alive as eras pass. Solving these mysteries can become national obsessions. Sometimes it's because people simply want a happy ending for everyone involved. Maybe they like knowing that being royal is no protection from crime or danger. Or maybe they just like solving mysteries.

Much of the fascination with mysteries is in the challenge of figuring out how to solve them—and some mysteries have been shrouded in conjecture and lack of hard evidence for so long that all kinds of stories and theories have developed, making it more and more difficult to separate truth from fiction.

But today we don't have to rely on guesswork or worry so much about how to weed out rumors and baseless theories. Thanks to the accurate and precise crime-solving techniques of forensics, many very old mysteries involving some of history's most famous people have been solved recently. Other royal riddles, however, stubbornly remain unsolved. As forensics techniques become more advanced, even these lingering mysteries may be unraveled … but only time will tell. For now, prepare to step into a world of majesty, mystery, and discovery.

Royals Time Line

ROYAL	BIRTH	DEATH
King Tut	ca 1341	1323 BCE
Kan Maax	ca 760	800
Louis XIII	1601	1643
Louis XIV	1638	1715
The Man in the Iron Mask	?	1703
Louis XVI	1754	1793
Napoleon Bonaparte	1769	1821
Louis XVII	1785	1795
Grand Duchess Anastasia	1901	1918
King Rama VIII	1925	1946
King Rama IX	1927	

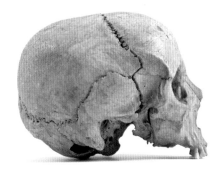

Forensics Time Line

ca 540 BCE First recorded archaeological dig. Led by Nabonidus, King of Babylon.

44 BCE First forensic autopsy. Showed that although Julius Caesar was stabbed by many knives, it was the second knife wound that killed him.

ca 1450 Archaeology. Developed as a science when Italian researchers became interested in ancient Greece.

1670 Single-lens microscope. Invented by Dutch scientist Antonie van Leeuwenhoek. It would become an important tool in analyzing evidence.

1812 World's first detective force. Sûreté Nationale is set up in Paris, France.

1835 Matching the bullet to the gun. Henry Goddard, a British police officer, studies markings on bullets and shows how a bullet can be matched to the gun that fired it.

1836 Arsenic test. Created by chemist James Marsh of Britain to detect very small amounts of arsenic in human tissue or body fluid.

1843 Mug shots. Belgian police begin taking photos (called mug shots) of criminals.

1846 Advanced autopsy technique. Rudolf Virchow, a professor in Germany, develops the specific, standardized autopsy technique still in use today.

1849 Forensic dental records. An American murder victim, reduced to bone fragments and a set of false teeth, is positively identified by a dentist, resulting in the conviction of the murderer.

1861 Hair as evidence. Virchow studies the importance of hair as evidence in a crime. He becomes known as the father of modern pathology.

1887 Deductive reasoning. *A Study in Scarlet*, the first book featuring Sherlock Holmes, is published. Holmes is known for using deductive reasoning (the process of drawing conclusions based on carefully analyzing available evidence) to solve crimes and is the world's most popular fictional detective.

1892   Fingerprinting. Police officer Juan Vucetich of Argentina makes the first criminal identification using fingerprints.

1890s   Crime scene forensics. Detectives begin gathering and analyzing crime scene evidence—such as fingerprints, hair, and items left behind—to solve crimes. Many years later, police would also be able to scientifically examine bloodstains and ballistics, DNA, and more.

1894   Handwriting analysis. A famous French court case involves deciding whether or not the accused army captain wrote a memo giving away his country's military secrets.

1895   X-rays. German physicist Wilhelm Conrad Röntgen discovers X-rays. They can be used to determine cause of death or to see inside objects without harming them.

1901   Blood type identification. Austrian-American biologist Karl Landsteiner helps devise a blood-typing test. Forensic scientists use the test to identify bloodstains at crime scenes.

1901   Human vs. animal blood test. Paul Uhlenhuth, a German scientist, creates a test to distinguish human blood from animal blood at crime scenes.

1910   First crime lab in the world. Opened in Lyons, France, by police detective Edmond Locard. He devises a basic principle of forensic science: "Every contact leaves a trace." Locard becomes known as the French Sherlock Holmes. He also shows how microscopes can reveal details that can be used to solve crimes.

1913   Identifying bullets. French forensics professor Victor Balthazard describes how bullet markings make each bullet unique.

1933   Dermal nitrate test. Developed in Mexico. Identifies gunshot residue on skin.

1974   Computed tomography (CT) scan. First used to give doctors detailed images of the internal organs of living patients. Later used to give similar information about crime victims.

1984   DNA analysis. British geneticist Alec Jeffreys is the first to use deoxyribonucleic acid (DNA) analysis to solve crimes.

TERROR IN THE JUNGLE

How Did an Entire Maya Royal Family Die?

CRIME SCENE

May 2005, remote rain forest of Guatemala

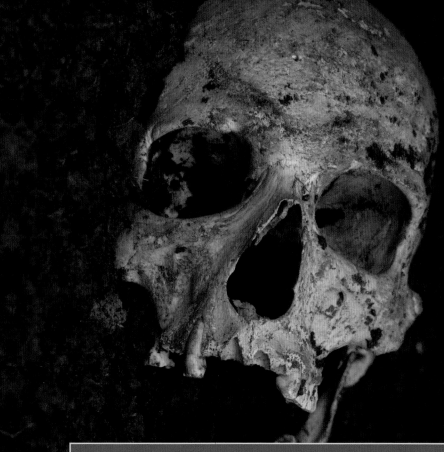

Crime-Solvers' Arsenal: Archaeology

People have been excavating the ruins and remains of earlier societies for thousands of years. But it wasn't until about 600 years ago that the study of human history and society through bones, artifacts, and other remains became the science of archaeology. That's when Flavio Biondo, an Italian historian, wrote a precise guide to the ruins of ancient Rome.

Forensic anthropology is the analysis of human remains to determine how a victim died. It was developed in 1850, when American doctor Jeffries Wyman examined charred bone fragments to help identify a murder victim and bring a criminal to justice.

Both forensic archaeology and forensic anthropology can tell a lot about how people lived—and how they died ...

The Mystery: A Grisly Discovery

Red macaws screeched overhead as the diggers worked deep in the heart of Guatemala's most remote rain forest. Swarms of buzzing, biting insects almost drowned out the roar of the howler monkeys swinging through the trees. It was only May, but the heat hung like a haze in the thick, dank air.

Two Guatemalan archaeologists were working alongside their staff. Suddenly, one of the scientists gave a strangled cry. Even the jungle noises seemed to stop for a moment. Then all the workers stared in horror. The pit where they were digging was at last revealing its shocking secret.

It was full of bones. Thousands and thousands of them.

Bone Identification 101

Whom did the bones belong to? Were they human bones?

Carefully, the workers began examining their grisly find. Some of the bones were thin and fairly straight. The archaeologists knew that nonhuman bones are usually heavier and more curved than these. Bones that the archaeologists identified as foot bones formed a long, narrow shape, like a human foot. Other animals, such as bears, cats, and dogs, tend to have wide feet.

Most nonhuman skulls have a pointed, elongated face and no chin. But these skulls each had a jawbone with a chin and a flat face. The eye sockets were also at the front of the face, not on the side like most animals'. Anthropologists believe that creatures needed eyes that would let them see straight ahead if they were to walk upright.

There was no doubt. These were human bones. But whose?

The History: Collapse of the Maya

When the scientists realized there were likely more than 30 skeletons buried there, they were shocked. They found shards of pottery that dated the grave back to 800 CE.

In 2005, when the scientists made their gruesome discovery, the site was in the middle of a thick jungle. But 1,200 years earlier, this pit had been part of a vast palace in Cancuén, one of the richest, most important cities in the ancient Maya empire. The bodies lying in the huge grave were likely Maya.

For hundreds of years, the Maya people, who lived in present-day Belize, El Salvador, Guatemala, Honduras, and Mexico, have been shrouded in mystery. Their civilization, one of the most intriguing ancient empires, likely began around 2600 BCE.

The Maya were a remarkably skilled people. They developed astronomy, calendars, and hieroglyphs; built elaborate temples and palaces; and were skilled farmers, weavers, and potters. But if they were so brilliant and talented, why did much of their civilization disappear?

Today, there are only about 7 million Maya still living in the same areas as their ancestors. But the vast, advanced empire mysteriously collapsed around 900 CE. Many of its amazing technological advances were lost forever.

Was there a link between the bodies of the Maya lying in the pit and the puzzling end of the Maya civilization? Who were these Maya, and why had their bodies just been tossed together in a mass grave? How had they died, and why?

The Clues: Bones Tell Their Stories

Despite the team's experience and expertise, they realized they needed help to answer their questions about the huge grave. They called in forensic scientists from the Guatemalan Forensic Anthropology Foundation. These experts were used to dealing with the horrors of modern mass murders and war crimes. But the science skills they'd learned to identify recent murderers and criminals might help solve this ancient mystery. The forensic scientists knew that bones can reveal the identity of dead people and give clues about their lives and deaths.

READING
THE BONES

Forensic archaeologists can tell whether bones belonged to men or women, adults or children. How can they tell the difference? There's quite a contrast between male and female pelvic bones. That's the large, slightly bowl-shaped bone at the bottom of the spine. Compared to a man's pelvis, a woman's tends to be flatter, more rounded, and larger, to allow her to give birth.

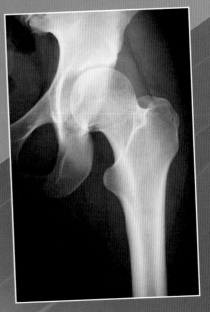

Most men also have thicker and longer bones in their arms, legs, hands, and feet. Female rib cages are narrower, and their shoulder blades are more rounded. Men tend to have bigger teeth than women, and the features on their skulls, such as the eyebrow ridge, also tend to be larger.

Children's bones aren't only smaller than adults' bones, but also the ends of the bones look different. Children's bones are still growing, and that growth takes place at the ends. Babies have a number of bones that aren't yet fused together, as they will when they grow older. Some bones of the skull and spine are separate in babies, and this gave the researchers a good idea of the age of some of the Maya victims.

The mix of male and female bones indicated these victims likely hadn't died in war on a battlefield. If they had, the forensic scientists reasoned, the bones would be mostly male. What made the mass grave even more gruesome was that some of the bones were children's. It was obvious the people found there hadn't died of old age.

The crew of Arthur Demarest, the anthropologist who was one of the team's leaders, could tell the bones in the grave had belonged to strong and healthy people. This told the scientists a number of facts. For one thing, it meant the people hadn't died of disease. They'd also had lots to eat, and eating well takes money. This finding led experts to conclude the bones likely belonged to Maya royalty, who could afford to eat lots of healthy, nutritious food.

More evidence pointed to a royal connection. Not only had the bones been found on a palace site, but also scattered throughout the grave were exquisite necklaces made from jade (more valuable to the Maya than gold), shells, and other priceless items.

Large, heavy rings of bronze and copper were also strewn about. Thick gold and silver bangles gleamed in the sun. Even more breathtaking, a fantastic jaguar-tooth necklace lay among the bones. The archaeologists knew all these materials were extremely precious to the Maya, and only the wealthiest could afford them.

Another clue confirmed the sovereign connection. The skulls of the children were oddly shaped. Their foreheads were pushed back, and each skull was long and slender, almost like a cob of corn. The archaeologists knew some Maya reshaped their children's skulls to resemble corn cobs. Soon after a royal baby was born, her head was bound between planks to mold it into an elongated shape. This was the Maya way of honoring the vegetable important to their culture. But only royal families were allowed to alter their babies' skulls like this. The researchers concluded that the bones in the grave definitely belonged to royalty.

The scientists had identified the bones as belonging to nobles. Could the experts make the bones reveal their secrets of how these royals had died?

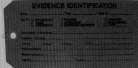

EVIDENCE IDENTIFICATION

The tiled pool in Guatemala where thousands of bones were found. Potsherds that were also discovered here allowed scientists to date the bones. Valuable jewelry found with the bones showed they belonged to Maya royals.

Violence in the jungle

Through days of drenching rain and scorching sun, the archaeologists and forensic scientists examined the bones more closely. Some were sliced completely in two. Other marks suggested the bones had been severed and hacked, as in battle. Spearheads and axe blades found in the grave were the likely weapons. These were the kinds of weapons found on a battlefield. But this grave contained royal men and women, boys and girls. It wasn't full of soldiers who had died at war.

How else might these nobles have died? The scientists were well aware of the Maya reputation for sacrificing people to their gods. But they also knew the Maya offered human sacrifices less often than was once believed, and that sacrifices were performed

GODS AND SACRIFICE

When most people think of the Maya, they imagine the sacrifices of humans and animals these ancient people made to their gods. No wonder—some of the ritual sacrifice methods were extremely gruesome. A victim might be held down by four helpers while his heart was ripped out. Or he might be shot to death with arrows, whipped until he died, or hurled off a high building. Priests and other leaders would also slice their own tongues or ears and use the blood to purify buildings.

Whom did the Maya sacrifice? After a successful battle, they would sacrifice prisoners to whatever god they had prayed to before the fight. To dedicate a temple or other structure, children were sacrificed. At the end of some ballgames, the loser might not just lose the match— he might lose his life, too! Maya gave sacrifices to more than 70 gods, including ones for everything from eclipses and medicine, to bees and death.

You might think that the Maya didn't value human life, but researchers think this likely isn't true. Instead, experts now believe that the Maya thought their gods required human sacrifice to maintain the order of the universe.

EVIDENCE IDENTIFICATION

The bones of Kan Maax in their separate, shallow grave. An engraved necklace and traces of a feathered headdress helped scientists identify the Maya king.

with great respect and ritual. It was clear to the anthropologists that these royals had been hurriedly killed and thrown into the mass grave. As well, there were far too many victims. This was no human sacrifice.

Yet another strange thing about the bones puzzled the scientists. They'd never seen ancient bones so well preserved out in the wild. Usually they lasted just a few years, not many centuries. The jungle's acidic soil, dampness, heat, and insects turned buried bones to dust.

How had these bones managed to persist after all this time? It was soon clear that the pit in which the bones lay was actually a sacred pool. It was larger and deeper than most modern backyard pools and was lined with tiles. Mud and water had covered the bones and protected them from the jungle's destruction.

Why would someone poison a ritual pond? Who would dispose of so many bodies so callously?

More mystery

It was hard to believe, but this dig site held another big surprise for the researchers. Not far from the mass grave they found a smaller one, holding a single man. The hole was shallow, as shallow as a grave the Maya typically dug for someone they valued as little as a beggar.

But this was no pauper. Green, red, and white lines around the man suggested he'd been buried wearing a headdress of feathers from a quetzal bird. The archaeologists knew that in Maya culture, only nobles could own these exquisite plumes.

What can the color and type of feathers found on a body say about the status of the dead person?

This feathered headdress stretched from the man's head to his feet. A shell necklace was etched with Maya writing, or glyphs. Painstakingly, the archaeologists deciphered the symbols. Then they gasped. The necklace identified this long-dead king as Kan Maax, the last ruler of Cancuén. Since the researchers had concluded the skeletons in the mass grave were those of royalty, the bones almost certainly belonged to Kan Maax's family and other nobles.

Kan's grave mystified the researchers. Although he'd been buried in an unmarked beggar's grave, his body had been carefully laid out and treated with respect. On the other hand, the burial seemed sudden and rushed.

How had Kan and the other royals died? The researchers were forced to accept a shocking conclusion: murder. They imagined the horrible scene and the innocent victims …

What was that sound? Kan Maax stopped in the hallway, listening intently. He was sure he'd heard something. Who was outside in the darkness, and what did they want?

For months, Kan had heard whispers of an impending attack. He'd ordered a thick wall built to protect his palace. The

barricade was almost complete, but he feared it wouldn't be finished soon enough.

Suddenly, a scream echoed through the palace, then another and another! Kan started running. He had to find his family! But servants were scrambling through the halls in blind panic. Pots and bowls clattered across the floors as commoners and royals ran, desperate to escape.

Across the grand hall ahead, Kan saw one of his young nephews running, his eyes wide with terror. Shadowy figures grabbed the boy from behind, stabbed him, and tossed him aside. Others threw spears at their victims and hacked them with axes.

Then the attackers saw Kan.

Within seconds, he was completely surrounded, his hands pulled roughly behind his back. Then Kan was dragged outside, to the edge of the sacred pool, just in front of the palace. His wife and children were already there, howling in fear. Soon, all the members of the royal family were gathered by the pond, crying and wailing.

At a signal, their captors raised their lances and killed Kan and the rest of Cancuén's ruling family. Most of the royals were simply shoved into the pool. The killers threw their weapons in after the murdered victims.

But Kan Maax was king and deserved better treatment than the rest of his family. Near the ritual pool, the murderers dug a shallow grave. They laid Kan's body in it, adorned with shell necklaces and a ceremonial feathered headdress.

The attackers weren't finished yet. By polluting the sacred pond with the royals' bodies, they'd poisoned and killed the water. Now they set about "murdering" the rest of the site. They chipped off the faces of all the stone carvings. Then they pushed over monuments, leaving them lying facedown in the broken rock.

After savagely destroying the carvings, the attackers ran off into the night, taking nothing from their victims or the palace, not even the lavish jewelry.

Over time, the jungle began to grow over the pool, the palace, and its surroundings. Over the next 100 years, the entire Maya empire collapsed. Kan Maax and the other nobles lay beneath the earth, the mystery of their deaths a secret. It wasn't long before no one remembered they were even there …

The archaeologists shivered despite the heavy jungle heat, then slowly resumed their digging. Now they had two mysteries to solve: Why had Kan Maax and the other royals been murdered, and why had the nobles been thrown into this special pool? They would have to try to solve this long-ago crime using only the site's bones and artifacts for clues.

The Suspects: Who Wanted the King Dead?

The researchers also wondered who was responsible for such a strange and gruesome act. They drew up a list of murder suspects and their motives, then began to consider the evidence for and against each one.

Was it a peasant uprising?

The common people who lived in Cancuén were the most logical suspects. For years, they had paid high taxes to support the royal family. Had Kan Maax and his family flaunted their wealth once too often before the starving commoners? And that jaguar necklace found among the bones—the danger involved in obtaining those fangs made the jewelry unbelievably expensive.

What about the vast palace where the royal family lived? It sprawled over an area larger than five football fields. It stood three stories high and included two hundred rooms and eleven court-yards. And, of course, it had its own sacred pool along one edge. Had the royals' extravagance caused their citizens' resentment to boil over into a vicious revolt?

The archaeologists knew the period when the massacre took

place was a time of great upheaval in the Maya culture. The rituals that had once enthralled the commoners no longer impressed them. Even Kan knew his empire was collapsing.

The worst drought in centuries had driven the common people from their homes in search of food. Thousands of peasants were on the move throughout the entire Maya empire. A throng of starving commoners could have swarmed into Kan Maax's vast palace in search of food and anything else they could grab, such as jewelry and money.

There was just one problem with this solution to the mysterious massacre: all that expensive jewelry left behind in the mass grave, strewn among the bones. Starving peasants would have been sure to rob their victims and then sell the valuables for food. Since these riches had been left with the nobles, it was unlikely commoners were the murderers.

So the scientists considered other possible suspects and motives.

Did a rival city kill the royals?

Cancuén was much more than just a city. It was what is known as a city-state, meaning it was as small as a city but as powerful as a whole country. Its ruler, Kan Maax, was considered a king.

Although Cancuén was in the middle of the jungle, it was at the junction of some major Maya trade routes. The city was always bustling with markets, traders, and deals. All of this business made it rich and the envy of less prosperous cities. How jealous were the rulers of those other cities? Were they resentful enough to resort to murder?

The ruler of every kingdom tried to outdo the others, building bigger temples and more elegant palaces, and staging more elaborate ceremonies. All of this required workers. Paying them could be expensive; frequently, one leader sent his soldiers to defeat another, then forced the conquered foes to work as slaves.

Soldiers would have had the weapons and the skills to kill all of the victims. But, like commoners, the soldiers usually stripped

Valuables found in the tiled pools indicated that the massacre victims hadn't been robbed. Carved jade and jaguar fangs were so expensive they could only be owned by the very wealthy.

their victims of any valuables. And if Kan's palace in Cancuén had been attacked by soldiers fighting for a jealous rival, they would have taken over the residence and the trade route. Instead, Kan's home was abandoned.

The archaeologists decided they would have to keep looking for other likely perpetrators.

Were jealous nobles behind the deadly crime?

Last on the archaeologists' list of murder suspects were Kan's own relatives. And he had a lot of them. His father, Taj Chan Ahk, had built a vast, powerful domain by marrying the daughters of other Maya kings. That bound the kings and their kingdoms to him. Taj's multiple wives all had children, and these sons and daughters also had children. By the time Kan came to the throne, the royal family was huge: it filled the 200-room royal palace.

THE FACE OF MYSTERY

More scientists have joined the team of detectives, including some who can figure out how old artifacts are by examining their atomic structure using a method called isotope analysis. Lasers are also being used to carefully clean the surface of bones to allow scientists to see them more clearly.

Today, scientists can use computerized three-dimensional facial reconstruction to show how the victims may have looked, based on the size and shape of their skull. It may be possible one day to look into the eyes of Kan Maax and his sons and daughters.

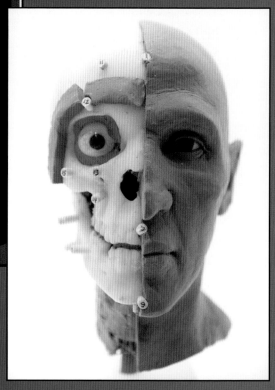

Even before Kan became king, there were power struggles within the many branches of Maya aristocracy. Each royal worked against the others to increase his own prestige and power. These greedy lords also tried to pressure Kan. Rituals and ceremonies no longer ensured their loyalty. They demanded jade, shells, exotic quetzal feathers, and more. A king who didn't keep up with the demands of his relatives often found they turned against him.

But somehow the archaeologists couldn't quite cast grasping nobles as Kan's killers. Usually after an invasion like the one Kan's family had endured, the attacking lords took over the site. First, they moved into the palace and stole any jewels and valuables they could find. Then they put someone on the throne and erected monuments in their own honor.

Not this time. After killing these royals, the murderers had tossed them into the holy pond, and then they'd savagely destroyed the rest of the site. It was unlikely the murderers were jealous, power-hungry nobles.

The Verdict: Expert Opinion

Arthur Demarest believes the mass killings were likely carried out by soldiers from another city-state but says more research is needed. The bones of the murder victims were only found in 2005, and a lot of evidence still needs to be analyzed. Probably much more is still buried, waiting to be discovered.

When the palace excavation site is bathed in sunlight, warm and bright, it's easy to imagine Kan and his family in their beautiful robes and exotic jewelry. It's not hard to picture them talking and laughing, totally unaware of the terrible fate awaiting them.

DEADLY EXILE

Was Emperor Napoleon Bonaparte Poisoned?

CRIME SCENE

May 5, 1821, Saint Helena Island, South Atlantic Ocean

Crime-Solvers' Arsenal: Autopsy

One of the most important techniques detectives use to figure out how someone died is an autopsy. It's the examination of a corpse to reveal what killed the victim, when, and more. Probably the first forensic autopsy was performed in 44 BCE, when the famous Roman leader Julius Caesar was stabbed to death by rival politicians. Doctors could tell that it was the second knife wound that actually killed Caesar.

However, it took almost 2,000 years for a scientific autopsy technique to be developed, and that process is still used today. Since leaders and royals continue to be murdered, forensic autopsy continues to be an important tool for solving royal mysteries.

The Mystery: Diagnosis Unknown

The howling wind and the pounding waves all around the island could drive a person mad. Napoleon, who'd once been undisturbed by the uproar and commotion of great armies, now desperately tried to cover his ears. He stumbled into his quarters, away from the prying eyes of his English guards and the pitiless wind and sea. Then this former emperor bent almost double in pain. His butlers exchanged glances as they tried to support him. Was this the end of one of the most famous men in history?

In 2004, a team of Italian and American doctors stated Napoleon must have died from an unfortunate and deadly combination of drugs his doctors had given him. In 2007, Dr. Patrick Kintz, a toxicologist (a scientist who studies poison), claimed that Napoleon had been murdered, poisoned with arsenic. That same year, a group of American, Canadian, and Swiss researchers insisted that the emperor had died of stomach cancer.

Two years later, a Danish doctor who is a leader in kidney research said that he had solved the puzzle. No question about it: Napoleon had died of kidney disease.

How did Napoleon die? Was he murdered? If so, who did it, and how?

The History: Guts and Glory

Napoleon was born in 1769 on the tiny French island of Corsica, in the Mediterranean Sea, between France and Italy. He trained as an artillery officer, which meant he was in charge of the soldiers who used cannons and similar weapons.

Enemies of Napoleon started a rumor that many people still believe: that he was very short. Actually, he was about 1.69 metres (5 feet 6 inches) tall, which was an average height for a man at the time. Napoleon was a brilliant military leader: energetic, determined, and amazingly successful in battle. In 1799, a few years

Napoleon wasn't born rich or to an upper-class family. But he became emperor of France, and ruled from 1804 to 1815. "I can no longer obey," he once said. "I have tasted command, and I cannot give it up."

after monarchy was abolished in France at the end of the French Revolution, Napoleon seized control of the country. By 1804, he was able to proclaim himself emperor of France.

But he wasn't satisfied. The thirst for power led him on a campaign to conquer all of Europe. Victory followed victory, until 1812, when he invaded Russia. A group of countries, including Russia, the United Kingdom, and Spain, banded together to defeat Napoleon. Not only was he forced to give up the throne of France, but also, in 1814, he was exiled to the Italian island of Elba.

A skilled military commander, Napoleon conquered most of Europe. That made him many enemies in other countries. Could one of them have tried to kill him?

Exile, part 1

You might think exile would have ended all Napoleon's ideas of conquest. But as emperor he had once claimed, "The word *impossible* is not in my dictionary."

To fight off boredom, Napoleon planned ways to develop Elba's iron mines. He also built up a small navy and army. In February 1815, just about 10 months after landing on the island, he was sailing back to France, ready to resume his conquering ways.

When Napoleon landed in France, he had an army of only 1,000 soldiers, but he was ready to gamble everything to be emperor again. Boldly, he approached a French fort, even though it was full of armed soldiers ready to shoot him to defend their country against him.

Napoleon marched out in front of his troops and shouted to the fort's defenders, who had their guns trained on him. "Soldiers!"

he yelled. "If there is one among you who wishes to kill his emperor, he can do so. Here I am! Kill your emperor, if you wish!"

The soldiers were amazed and impressed at such boldness. Instead of killing Napoleon then and there, they joined him. The growing army marched to Paris, France's capital. Soon, Napoleon was emperor again and was ready to begin another attempt to become the ruler of all of Europe.

But the other countries were better prepared this time. When Napoleon and his forces marched on to Belgium, they were defeated at the famous Battle of Waterloo on June 18, 1815.

Europe's other kings and emperors wanted to make sure Napoleon would never go to battle again. The former emperor felt he should be allowed to live a life of ease in England as a country gentleman. But that wasn't far enough from France for his opponents. Instead, he was sent to the island of Saint Helena.

Exile, part 2

Napoleon spent a lot of time on the shore of Saint Helena, staring out to sea. All he saw was ocean and more ocean. In vain, he scanned the horizon, hoping to spot a French ship coming to rescue him from exile and restore him to the throne and country he loved.

The ship never came. Instead, Napoleon paced the beach helplessly on one of the most isolated islands in the world. Far out in the middle of the south Atlantic Ocean, midway between South Africa and South America, lay damp, foggy Saint Helena. Smaller than many cities, this tropical island was windswept and wet.

The man who once said, "I should have conquered the world," was now a prisoner on a tiny, remote island. English guards watched Napoleon's every move to make sure he didn't escape. However, he was allowed about 20 servants and aides, including his most trusted servant and valet, Louis Marchand, and he ate elaborate, fattening meals off the best French china.

Napoleon spent six cold, damp, lonely years on Saint Helena. He hated being watched by the English guards and officials. As

Napoleon hated being exiled on lonely Saint Helena Island. "Death is nothing," he said, "but to live defeated and inglorious is to die daily." His attitude may have contributed to his death.

time went by, he spent less and less time outside in the gardens and more inside, hiding behind shutters and blinds.

Napoleon's despair, along with the endless damp and cold, would have taken its toll on any man. No one was surprised that by February 1821, Napoleon's health had become very poor. Marchand described in his diary how his employer complained of terrible stomach pains and the doctors could do nothing to relieve them. On May 5, far from the thousands who had once bowed to him, the great emperor died and was buried on Saint Helena.

Three times as many books have been written on Napoleon than on any other historical character, which makes him the most written-about person ever. His battles and campaigns are still dissected in military academies all over the world. Despite all this research and study, no one knows for sure how this incredible man died.

The Clues: Dead Men Do Tell Tales

What would eventually help solve the mystery was a great stroke of historical luck. Before Napoleon was buried, doctors performed an autopsy on his body. The word *autopsy* comes from a Greek word that means "to see for oneself." Today, a specialized surgeon known as a pathologist performs autopsies to identify signs of disease, injury, and even murder. Modern autopsies yield so much vital information that they've become a standard tool for crime-solvers. But when Napoleon died, autopsies were rare.

If the cause of death is unknown, the pathologist will check for bullets, cuts, or other symptoms of blows to the corpse. She may also look for indications of poison and drugs. Blood, urine, and even fluid in the eye can show signs of medicine and other drugs, alcohol, or chemicals.

Pathologists may carefully check the digestive system for poison. Any food remaining there can tell experts clues about the person's last meal and when it was eaten. For instance, it usually takes a little more than a day to digest a meal, but that speed can be affected by illness, drugs, fear, and more.

Pathologists also check the external surfaces of a body for evidence. Is the skin bruised, or does it have dirt on it that could show the victim was dragged? Do hair samples show the use of drugs or poisons? Do scrapings from under the fingernails show that a victim might have fought an attacker? The doctors also look for such things as gunshot residue, fibers, and paint chips.

Ice-cold and stiff

One of the first things police officers do when they arrive at the scene of a murder is try to estimate how long the victim has been dead. That information could help the officers determine whether the person was alone, where she had been, or where she might have been going.

Detectives at the crime scene can make a general judgment

THE EYES HAVE IT

Eyes can also tell pathologists about the time of death. A thin, cloudy film forms over the eyes within three hours of a victim dying. Doctors know that a dead person has less fluid pressure behind his eye than a live person, and that makes the eyeball softer. The amount of softness can give clues about the time of death.

ANTS, COCKROACHES, AND FLIES

If a dead body has been abandoned outside for more than a day, forensic scientists analyze the insects found in it to try to determine the time of death. Some bugs will feed and lay their eggs only on a corpse, and scientists know how long the eggs take to hatch.

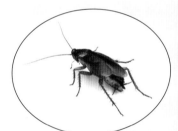

Depending on what insects are found and where they are in their life cycle, pathologists can tell how long the person has been dead. For instance, flies may begin to feed on a dead body and lay their eggs almost immediately after the victim is killed. Ants and cockroaches don't show up for one to two weeks. Beetles and mites are found after three or four weeks.

about the time of death by the temperature of the body and its stiffness. However, a pathologist can be more accurate. He uses a mathematical formula that includes the temperature of the body, the temperature at the scene of the crime, the victim's weight, and more. Humidity, air movement, and the amount of fat on the body also affect how fast a corpse cools after death.

The stiffening of a dead body is called rigor mortis, and it happens as the body's muscles harden due to a lack of blood and oxygen. The victim's eyelids and jaw stiffen first, and then within six to twelve hours the entire body shows rigor mortis. The process reverses itself, and the body becomes flexible again after another six to twelve hours.

The color of death

Pathologists know that a body also changes color after death. When the heart stops pumping, blood stops moving, so thanks to gravity, blood pools in the points of the body that are the lowest.

About two days after a victim has died, bacteria start breeding on the skin, and that gives the victim a greenish tinge. Then, between four and seven days after a victim has died, her skin begins to look like marble. That's because the veins in the body come closer to the surface and become more visible.

Napoleon's autopsy

Nowadays, an autopsy takes around four to six hours. When Napoleon died, more than 200 years ago, his autopsy took much less time. Doctors didn't know nearly as much about examining dead bodies as they do now. They weren't aware of just how much a corpse can tell about how the person lived and died.

But in Napoleon's case there was another, more urgent, reason why his autopsy was rushed. Because of Saint Helena's tropical temperatures, Napoleon's body quickly began to stink. The doctors couldn't stand the stench. No wonder they tried to complete the grisly job as quickly as possible.

François Carlo Antommarchi, Napoleon's personal doctor, was the main doctor performing the autopsy. He noted there was a deep corrosion of the former emperor's stomach lining and a growth at its base. From this, he concluded Napoleon had died of stomach cancer.

Antommarchi also made a note of the surprising lack of hair on Napoleon's body, but either the doctor didn't know that this might indicate a particular type of poisoning, or he didn't want to suggest the former emperor might have been murdered.

Napoleon's British guards liked the diagnosis of stomach cancer because nobody could blame or accuse them of not taking good care of their important prisoner. Nevertheless, although it was Antommarchi who autopsied Napoleon's body and declared he had died of stomach cancer, he refused to sign official papers stating this finding. "What had I to do with … English reports?" he asked.

Was that the real reason, or did Antommarchi not want to sign his name to what he knew was a lie? Had he rushed through his foul-smelling job and missed a vital symptom or clue?

Death by cancer?

Antommarchi couldn't have known it when he performed Napoleon's autopsy, but in 1938, a doctor with a special interest in the emperor discovered that Napoleon's father had died of the same disease Antommarchi had diagnosed.

Some types of stomach cancer are genetic, and there are doctors who believe this is the kind Napoleon had. Other researchers disagree. They say there's no way Napoleon died of stomach cancer because one of the disease's classic symptoms is that the patient loses a lot of weight. Napoleon was still plump when he died.

Murder by poison?

Napoleon had always suspected that he would be murdered. "Shall I tell you the truth, Sir?" he asked Sir Hudson Lowe, the British

DEAD MAN'S FLOAT

If a body is found in water, an autopsy can determine whether the person drowned or was dead before she hit the water. A victim likely drowned if she has water in her lungs, throat, and stomach, and if her lungs are swollen. Investigators may also find twigs and stones in the victim's hands, which show she tried to grab at things to save herself.

TOOLS OF THE TRADE

You might be surprised at the tools doctors use in an autopsy: pruning shears, bread knives, bone saws, and even large, heavy needles (to sew up the body after the examination). Pathologists don't use delicate surgical tools because they're not doing micro-surgery and they don't need to worry about nicking a blood vessel. Many of the instruments doctors use are quite rough and heavy and have changed very little over the past 100 years.

governor of Saint Helena. "Yes, Sir, shall I tell you the truth? I believe that you have received orders to kill me—yes, to kill me."

The rumor that Napoleon had been poisoned began in 1840, when his body was dug up to be moved from Saint Helena to Paris. The French officials and military personnel at the grave site were surprised to see the emperor's corpse unusually well preserved. It looked as if it had been in the ground for just a few days, not almost 20 years.

Arsenic, a poison, has been used as a preservative in taxidermy, the process of preparing dead animals for display. Did this poison account for the lack of decomposition of Napoleon's body?

At Napoleon's autopsy, samples of his hair had been taken and preserved. Actually, lots of hair samples were available to researchers. The former emperor gave out locks of his hair as gifts to people.

In the 1950s, a Swedish poisons expert obtained a sample of hair certified to have belonged to Napoleon and arranged for forensic scientists to test it. They were shocked by what they found. The hair contained remarkably high concentrations of arsenic: as much as 38 times the normal amount. That's easily more than enough to kill someone.

Even more notable, there were different amounts of the poison in different parts of the hair. This showed that the amount of arsenic in Napoleon's body had changed a lot from day to day. It proved he had been swallowing arsenic every day, which suggests it must have been given to him deliberately.

There were traces of arsenic in Napoleon's hair, but does that necessarily mean he was poisoned?

In Napoleon's day, arsenic was popular with murderers because it was tasteless and easy to get since it was used as a dye, as a face powder, and in hair products, medicines, and other everyday items. Though arsenic was common, investigators back then weren't able to detect it in a body. Modern experts suggest the poison was given to Napoleon slowly to make it look like he'd died of natural causes. But in Napoleon's dying days, he showed obvious symptoms of arsenic poisoning: weakness, stomach pain, and vomiting.

The Suspects: Whodunit?

If Napoleon was poisoned, the murderer had to be someone close enough to him to commit the crime. Other people living on Saint Helena ate the same food as Napoleon, and it would have been difficult for the killer to poison just Napoleon's food. If there was a murderer, that person had to be someone Napoleon trusted.

Did Napoleon's valet do it?

Napoleon's valet, Louis Marchand, had been his servant a long time, and there's no sign that he was not entirely trustworthy.

What about the butler?

The same cannot be said about Charles Tristan, marquis de Montholon, a sort of head butler to Napoleon. He had the opportunity to kill his employer—and plenty of motives, too.

How could Tristan have slipped arsenic into Napoleon's food? He likely didn't. Instead, he probably added it to his boss's wine. You see, Napoleon insisted on drinking a special wine on Saint Helena, one that only he drank. It was Tristan who poured this wine for the former emperor. It's true that no one ever saw Tristan (or anyone else) add anything to Napoleon's wine. But it would have been easy for the marquis to slip a little arsenic into his employer's glass each day.

Why would Tristan have poisoned Napoleon? Some historians say that the emperor had had an affair with Tristan's wife, so Tristan wanted him dead. Others say that Tristan was desperate to see his wife again. She'd sailed for Paris because she couldn't stand the isolation of Saint Helena any longer. If Tristan shortened Napoleon's life, he could join his wife back in France sooner.

An even stronger possible motive was money. Tristan knew that Napoleon planned to leave him a large inheritance to thank him for his service. Did he become tired of waiting for it? Or maybe it wasn't Napoleon's money Tristan wanted. Perhaps he was promised a hefty reward from the English or French government if he got rid of the troublesome prisoner.

Did Napoleon's wallpaper kill him?

Could a person poison himself without even knowing it? It is possible that Napoleon may have poisoned himself. It's surprising just how many ways he could have been exposed to arsenic. Winemakers, including Napoleon, although he only did it as a hobby, used arsenic to dry out their wine casks.

In 1982, a chemist suggested that Napoleon might have been poisoned by the wallpaper in his home on Saint Helena. When the wallpaper was analyzed, it was indeed found to contain arsenic. Saint Helena is a very damp island, and the wallpaper could easily have become moldy. That would have broken down the arsenic in the dye, releasing it into the air.

Napoleon spent a lot of time indoors in his final years because he hated the feeling that he was always being watched by his captors. Some experts say that's why he was poisoned by the wallpaper, while other people who lived there but went outside more often were not.

During Napoleon's time, it was also the fashion to use arsenic as a recreational drug. European thrill seekers claimed it made them feel better. Napoleon was bored in exile, and he might have deliberately taken arsenic. Of course, as his body became used to the drug, he had to take more and more to get the same effect.

Killer kidneys?

What about the theory that Napoleon died of kidney disease? This theory seems to fit the symptoms he showed throughout his life.

For instance, officers who served with him and knew him as a brilliant, energetic commander and strategist worried that at times Napoleon appeared sluggish and dull. These changes in him could have been symptoms of kidney disease. At the Battle of Waterloo, Napoleon's last battle and the one that resulted in his exile to Saint

NAPOLEON MYTH EXPOSED

Many portraits painted of Napoleon show him with his right hand hidden in his jacket. Over the years, people have suggested various reasons for the pose: he was massaging a painful ulcer, he had a deformed hand, artists aren't very good at painting hands, and more. Actually, the "hand-in-jacket" pose was used in paintings of all upper-class men in the time when Napoleon lived.

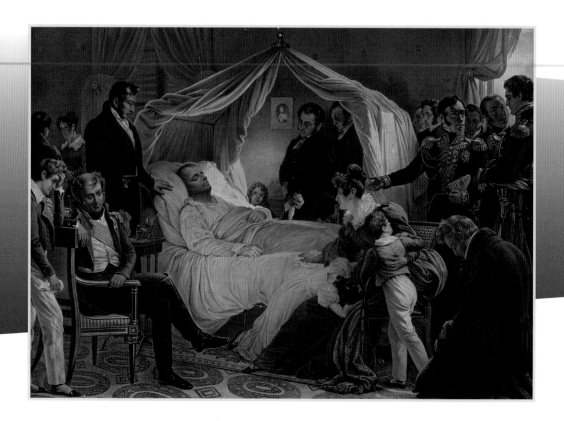

EVIDENCE IDENTIFICATION

Napoleon became very ill in February 1821, but he didn't die until early May. "It requires more courage to suffer," the former emperor said, "than to die."

Helena, the usually commanding leader was indecisive and sleepy. Some people think kidney disease could have caused the stomach corrosion that Antommarchi found during Napoleon's autopsy.

The Verdict: The Evidence Is in the Pants

Napoleon's story still captures people's imagination. At least 300,000 books have been written about him and the times he lived in. That's an average of approximately four books published every day since his death in 1821. Napoleon would have undoubtedly been pleased that people are still fascinated by his life. In fact, he probably expected it. "Even when I am gone, I shall remain in people's minds," he once said. "My name will be the war cry of their efforts, the motto of their hopes."

The theory that Napoleon died of arsenic poisoning was finally put to rest in 2008. Despite the large amount of arsenic in his hair, this poison was likely not the cause of his death. Many Europeans in Napoleon's time had a lot of arsenic in their bodies.

Experts in arsenic poisoning examined the samples of Napoleon's hair taken throughout his life—not just before his death—and hair from his family and others living at the same time. Their findings showed that even when Napoleon was a boy, he already had a lot of arsenic in his hair.

Most experts now agree that Napoleon died of stomach cancer, as his father had. It's true that Napoleon was quite fat when he died, unlike most cancer sufferers. But he actually had lost a lot of weight at the end of his life. Historians examined the shrinking waist measurements of his pants to prove this! Though Napoleon had lived all of his adult life knowing he had mortal enemies, it was disease, not murder, that ended the emperor's life.

IDENTITY UNKNOWN

Who Was the Man in the Iron Mask?

CRIME SCENE

November 19, 1703, Paris, France

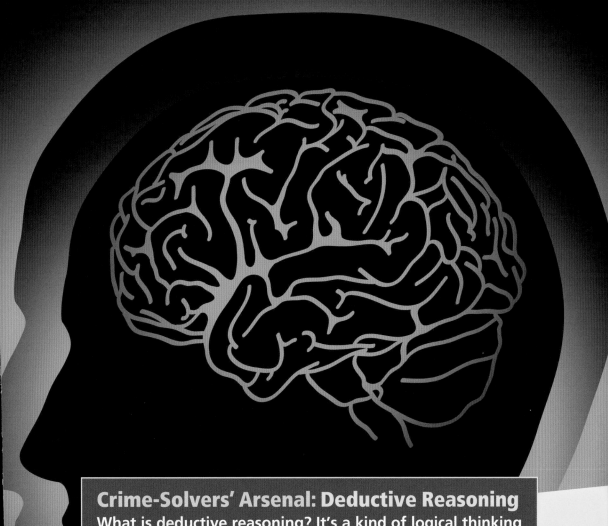

Crime-Solvers' Arsenal: Deductive Reasoning

What is deductive reasoning? It's a kind of logical thinking that's been around for centuries. But in the late 1890s, detectives began to use deductive reasoning to solve crimes. Imagine you walked into the kitchen and found your piece of chocolate cake gone. You'd want to figure out who had stolen it. If your brother was the only one in the house and looked guilty, you might deduce he'd eaten your cake, especially if he had chocolate crumbs all over his face.

Today, police use deductive reasoning to solve many crimes, including ones that have remained unsolved for a long time. These "cold cases" are sometimes hundreds of years old. One of the most fascinating cold cases of all is the tragic story of the Man in the Iron Mask.

The Mystery: A Very Peculiar Prisoner

"Get that stool out of here! Move that old bed! Out to the court-yard with it and burn it," yelled Bénigne d'Auvergne de Saint-Mars, governor of Paris's Bastille prison. "The prisoner's clothes, too! Now! What are you doing just standing there? I want every scrap of plaster pulled off all the walls! No trace must be left of the prisoner! Get to work, you lazy oafs!"

For years, Saint-Mars had worked hard to make sure no one discovered the true identity of the prisoner, the legendary Man in the Iron Mask. Every time the governor was promoted to a new prison elsewhere in France, the prisoner was moved along with him. That way, no new officials would have to be informed of the secret of his identity.

As few people as possible were supposed to know about the Man in the Iron Mask. Those orders came right from France's king, Louis XIV. The prisoner was forbidden to speak with anyone in case he dropped any clues to his past and identity.

On November 19, 1703, the Man in the Iron Mask finally died. But the prison's governor was taking no chances that the masked convict's identity would be revealed. In case he had managed to leave a message somewhere in his cell or on his furniture or clothes, everything would be destroyed or burned. That prisoner would not outsmart Saint-Mars now!

When the body of the Man in the Iron Mask was taken from the Bastille and buried, his name was recorded as Antonio Ercole Matthioli, age 45. If people knew his name, why was there any mystery about his identity?

For one thing, this prisoner had first been imprisoned in 1669, or 34 years earlier. But the death records stated he was 45 years old. That meant he was just 11 years old when he was first locked away. This was very unlikely because none of the stories written about the Man in the Iron Mask ever referred to him as a child. And the name? French prison staff often buried prisoners,

Many people believed the Man in the Iron Mask was of noble birth. So artists drew the mysterious figure with such luxuries as a lace tablecloth, a book—and even a cello.

especially ones who had anything to do with politics, under false names, usually Italian names. It's likely the dead man's name and age were completely made up. Obviously, the death records about this mysterious prisoner can't be trusted. Who was the Man in the Iron Mask, and why has the mystery of his identity intrigued people for hundreds of years?

The History: The Legend Begins

The story of the Man in the Iron Mask began in July 1669, when King Louis XIV of France had his soldiers arrest a man in Dunkirk, on the coast of northern France. The secretary of state wrote to Governor Saint-Mars: *You must never, under any pretenses, listen*

THE BASTILLE

The last prison where the Man in the Iron Mask was confined was the Bastille, in Paris. *Bastille* means "castle" in French. This prison held common criminals, such as forgers and swindlers, but also rich people and high-ranking officials.

The Bastille had a reputation for its sinister dungeons. There are stories of rats sharing the prisoners' beds of wet straw, meals of nothing but bread and water, and cells that were bone-chilling in winter. Some of the convicts were tortured and chained to the walls of their dark, damp cells.

If a prisoner survived his sentence and was finally released from the Bastille, he wasn't allowed to talk about his experiences there. Prisoners were forced to take a vow of silence before they were allowed to leave. No wonder rumors and stories sprang up about the horrors committed there. But actually, important or noble prisoners in the Bastille were treated well, fed the best food (and lots of it), and allowed to bring in their own comfortable furniture and even servants.

The prison where the Man in the Iron Mask languished didn't survive long after its famous prisoner died. When Parisians stormed the Bastille on July 14, 1789, they started the French Revolution, which changed the history of France. The building was mostly torn down later that year. Today, there are cafés and stores where this infamous prison once stood.

to what he may wish to tell you. You must threaten him with death if he speaks one word except about his actual needs.

From 1669 to 1681, Saint-Mars and his prisoner were in the Pignerol fortress. It's in southeastern France and is now part of Italy. Then Saint-Mars was moved to Exilles prison in the same area, and the Man in the Iron Mask was moved with him. (Some people say the gray stone jail is still haunted by this famous inmate, who silently stalks the hallways.)

Between 1687 and 1698, Saint-Mars and his masked prisoner were at a prison on the small, tree-covered island of Sainte-Marguerite, off the coast of southern France. Also imprisoned there were rebels, spies, and others who'd committed political crimes. Today, people can tour the cell where the Man in the Iron Mask is supposed to have been kept.

In 1698, Saint-Mars was promoted to governor of the Bastille, France's most infamous prison. Of course, the Man in the Iron Mask again moved with him. Despite what the burial records said, other records claim that by this point the prisoner was an old man. The Bastille would be his last home.

In all of these prisons, two musketeers, members of Louis XIV's special troop of soldiers, guarded the cell of the Man in the Iron Mask at all times, night and day. Their orders were to kill the prisoner if he removed his mask. The secretary of state had also said, "It is of the first importance that he is not allowed to tell what he knows to any living person."

The mystery behind the mask

Just imagine how it would feel to wear an iron face covering year after year and never take it off. It would have rusted quickly and made eating and bathing incredibly difficult. Infections would have set in where the iron rubbed against skin. Imagine trying to scratch an itchy nose or sneeze! Actually, the mask wasn't made of iron or any metal. The only solid evidence about the mask is from records kept by an official at the Bastille. He wrote that it was sewn of black velvet.

If a prisoner's face is hidden by a mask, what can that say about the prisoner? About the jailers?

King Louis XIV gave orders about the care of the Man in the Iron Mask and insisted the prisoner be carefully guarded. This led people to think that the convict must be someone very special.

And it likely wasn't a mask, either. The covering was probably more of a hood that cloaked much of the convict's face. And he probably didn't even wear it all the time. The masked prisoner only had to wear the hood when anyone entered his cell. He actually spent most of his time unmasked. However, the idea of a heavy iron mask caught people's imagination, and it was this frightening metal face that inspired writers, and later moviemakers, to keep the horrifying image of the Man in the Iron Mask alive.

The Man in the Iron Mask is said to have received very good treatment, which suggests the guards must have had reason to think he was from the upper class. He had access to expensive books, and prison records state that he requested and received good clothing and shirts edged in delicate lace.

For 300 years, people have tried to unravel the mystery of the Man in the Iron Mask. But there's no new evidence to work with. Does that mean the mystery can never be solved?

The Clues: Making Deductions

There may not be any new artifacts or physical clues about the identity of the Man in the Iron Mask, but there's still a useful tool researchers can use: deductive reasoning. It helps detectives weigh evidence, predict where a criminal might strike next, and of course, solve crimes. If you've ever played the game Clue, then you've used deductive reasoning to solve crimes.

People have always used deductive reasoning, but crime-solvers began to consider it a tool more than 120 years ago. Probably the most well-known detective to use this technique never did any real detecting—in fact, he didn't even exist. His name was Sherlock Holmes. The writer Sir Arthur Conan Doyle invented this world-famous detective.

Doyle had trained as a doctor, not as a detective, but one of his professors, Joseph Bell, was known for his skill at observation and deduction. Doyle modeled Holmes on Bell. Although Holmes only solved mysteries in books, not in reality, he taught detectives a lot about deductive reasoning.

How does deductive reasoning work? It involves two steps: gathering evidence and then assessing it.

Gathering evidence

Normally, evidence doesn't appear in any neat way. The evidence-collecting process can be difficult because the clues are rarely uncovered in the same order they fit in the story of the crime.

For instance, sometimes detectives find the footprints of the

DEDUCTIVE REASONING TODAY

Deductive reasoning can do more than solve crimes. During World War II, Britain and its allies used it to create a profile of Adolph Hitler, leader of Germany's Nazi forces, to try to anticipate what decisions he would make and where he might attack next. Today, deductive reasoning is used to catch serial killers, criminals in gangs, drug dealers, terrorists, and spies.

murderer as he fled the scene of the crime *before* they find the murder weapon or can figure out the time the murder took place. Usually, investigators turn up the evidence in random sequence, and then have to create a timetable that fits the facts. They take the facts and evidence and, almost like puzzle pieces, arrange them in the way that makes the most sense.

Detectives solving crimes by deductive reasoning often have to try to fill any holes that are obvious in the evidence. They may have to consider where or when more information might be available. Talking over a case with another detective can help an investigator come up with new ideas for obtaining information or additional witnesses to interview.

It's also important to make sure no information has been overlooked. For instance, in old records or letters, investigators need to carefully examine the backs of the pages or the margins. Are there any secret messages in the doodles at the top of the page or information written in code?

In the case of the Man in the Iron Mask, there's a lot of contradictory information. For instance, Princess Palatine, Louis XIV's sister-in-law, wrote in a letter in 1711, eight years after the masked prisoner had died, "No one has ever been able to find out who he was." But just two weeks later, she wrote that he was an English nobleman who had worked with the Duke of Berwick.

There was just one problem with this evidence. This Duke of Berwick wasn't born until 1670, or a year after the Man in the Iron Mask was known to already be imprisoned. A historian might assume the princess would have insider information because she was closely related to the king. But when her story is examined, it's likely she was as much in the dark as everyone else.

Princess Palatine may have made this mistake accidentally. But sometimes detectives find that witnesses deliberately try to lead them away from the truth to cover up crimes they committed or shield someone else. And sometimes what people *don't* say can be as interesting and useful as what they *do* say.

Assessing evidence

What can a hand-writing sample say about a criminal— or a victim?

Not only do detectives have to collect the evidence, but they also have to evaluate it. Is the information accurate, and can its source be trusted? Perhaps the person supplying the material has a reason to lie or to mislead the police.

Some records about the Man in the Iron Mask that should have been written by only one person are in different handwriting. What does this mean? When was the second person's handwriting added, and whose writing is it? It's yet another mystery surrounding the Man in the Iron Mask.

In the end, investigators often have to combine deductive reasoning with their gut reaction. For no particular reason, they may feel a witness is lying or that false evidence has been planted. It takes a lot of experience for a detective or historian to develop that sixth sense that tells them what evidence to review more closely and what records are worth examining one more time.

The Speculation: A Snob, Twins, and More

For hundreds of years, people have used deductive reasoning to try to identify the Man in the Iron Mask and why his face had to be kept a secret. Over the hundreds of years since the mystery around this man first began, many rumors, legends, and myths have sprung up to try to uncover the truth behind the mask.

Victim of scandal?

One theory about his identity involves France's king and queen, Louis XIII and Queen Anne. Back in the 1600s, it seemed odd to many in France that this royal pair had spent little time together over the 22 years of their marriage and that they had no children. Yet somehow, in 1638, the queen suddenly found herself pregnant.

Not surprisingly, rumors flew that Louis wasn't really the baby's father. And the boy, Louis XIV, was strong and handsome, not at all like his skinny, bumbling father. People speculated that

EVIDENCE IDENTIFICATION

Louis XIII and his wife, Queen Anne, were often separated by Louis's duties as king. Was Louis the father of the boy who became Louis XIV—or was the boy actually the son of the Man in the Iron Mask?

Louis XIV's real father had been persuaded or forced to leave the country, having provided the queen with a child and the French throne with an heir. But in 1669, the story goes, this father became homesick—or thought he could extort some money—and returned to France.

According to this theory, by the time the mystery father arrived home, the boy had become king. If news got out that he wasn't really Louis XIII's son, the young king would have been stripped of his power and wealth. He couldn't let his real father tell

the true story and expose Louis as illegitimate. There was no choice: the man had to be not only jailed, but also silenced.

But not everyone believed this story. After all, Louis XIV wasn't his parents' first and only child. Poor Queen Anne had given birth to four stillborn children, the last one just a few years before Louis XIV's birth. Despite what some may have thought, the king and queen obviously spent enough time together to have a child.

If Louis XIV was another man's child, many people would likely have known about it. At this time, the king of France was all-powerful in his country, but even so, he couldn't stop people from gossiping.

Double trouble

Another story suggested that when the queen finally gave birth to an heir to the throne, she actually produced twins. She and the king feared this would cause problems when Louis XIII died. Which twin should inherit the throne? Perhaps someone decided to make the decision easier by sending away one twin and bringing up the other to be king.

Having twins was unusual in the French royal family, and maybe Queen Anne also worried that she'd be considered odd. By getting rid of one twin immediately, she would have seemed more normal and prevented any question about which one should inherit the throne. Of course, the king and queen wouldn't want to kill their own child. But if the twin looked exactly like the future king, questions would be asked. Imprisoning the twin behind a mask might have seemed a good solution.

But how could such an outrageous deception be kept secret for so many years? Why are there no records anywhere about it? And would any parent willingly allow his child to be imprisoned?

Why did everyone assume that the Man in the Iron Mask was a close relative to France's king? More puzzling still—why wasn't he simply killed once he was imprisoned? Many prisoners in France and in other countries were never seen again once the jail doors clanged shut behind them. Killing anyone is a crime, but

WHO WAS MATTHIOLI, ANYWAY?

Was there a real person behind the name used on the death records of the Man in the Iron Mask? Antonio Ercole Matthioli was in fact an Italian politician, and not a very honest one. He was involved in negotiations between French and Italian nobles but ended up double-crossing them all.

It was the last time Matthioli would do anything that sneaky. The French government grabbed him and threw him into Pignerol prison, the first prison where the Man in the Iron Mask was held. But Matthioli wasn't imprisoned there until 1679, 10 years after the masked convict was recorded to be in prison.

What's more, what Matthioli had done was common knowledge in France. There seemed no point in masking him or keeping his identity secret. Unfortunately, the death certificate for the Man in the Iron Mask was destroyed in 1871 when the building where it was stored burned down. It isn't possible to examine the records for further information.

some murders are considered worse than others. Killing a king, or a family member such as a son or brother, is considered the worst kind of bloodshed. Even the all-powerful King Louis XIII would likely have hesitated to kill his own son.

Why might royalty imprison one of their own—in a mask?!

The Woman in the Iron Mask?

Some historians argue that the legendary masked prisoner wasn't a man at all! Some say she was the daughter of the queen—but the king was not her father, so she was illegitimate. If Queen Anne had had a daughter with a man who wasn't her husband, she may have tried to hide the little girl away. Why? If Louis knew the child wasn't his, he might have been furious, and Anne might have been scared of what he would do to her and her daughter.

Another story says the woman actually was the legitimate daughter of Louis XIII and Queen Anne. But the king and queen were disappointed she wasn't a boy and switched her for someone else's male baby, who became Louis XIV.

At that time in France, women were not allowed to inherit the throne, and if there were no male heir, the power would pass to another branch of the family. Switching a baby girl for a boy would have been one way Louis and Anne could have kept control.

But some experts say it's unlikely the Man in the Iron Mask was a woman. They point to the fact that there were other women in French prisons and in the Bastille. The prisoner could have been kept with them. And no one ever described the prisoner as looking like a woman. In fact, the prisoner was said to be quite tall and muscular. As well, the prisoner was an adult, not a child. Where had she been hidden before she was first recorded as being imprisoned in the Pignerol fortress in 1669?

A power struggle?

Another intriguing story claims that not only was the Man in the Iron Mask Louis's brother, but he also married while in prison and had a son. Apparently, the child was sent away to Corsica, a French

DON'T READ THIS!

One story about the Man in the Iron Mask tells how he once managed to get out a message. Some rumors say he scratched it on a silver plate; others that he wrote it in his blood on a shirt.

Apparently, the fisherman who found the message didn't know what it was. But he decided the only place the plate or shirt could have come from was the prison, so he brought it back there. The guards saw immediately that the note proclaimed the prisoner's identity. They were about to kill the fisherman to stop him from spreading the story. But he managed to gasp out the fact that saved him: he couldn't read and had no idea what the message said!

Artists tended to show the Man in the Iron Mask wearing expensive clothes, but no one is really certain what he wore. Even experts don't know if the prisoner was a royal, a commoner— or even a woman!

island southeast of France. Corsica is also the birthplace of the man who would become emperor of France and ruler over much of Europe in the early 1800s, Napoleon Bonaparte (see page 22).

This supposed royal son, some people believe, was an ancestor of Napoleon. The emperor desperately wanted this to be true, so when he was in power, he had investigators scour French royal records to prove it.

It's true Napoleon became an extraordinarily powerful man, unlike the rest of his family. Some people felt he must have inherited his sense of command and talent for leadership from royalty. But the emperor never found any definite evidence to support his claim. Nor did he find out anything else to identify the masked prisoner once and for all. There doesn't seem to be enough evidence to prove that The Man in the Iron Mask was Napoleon's grandfather.

Victim of blame?

What if the Man in the Iron Mask wasn't royal after all? After a lot of research, some historians think he was a convict listed in the prison records as Eustace Dauger, a butler. Investigators don't know what crime Dauger committed to result in imprisonment, but some suggest he might have been hired by the secretary of state to poison someone, but he messed up the job. His penalty was lifelong imprisonment and a mask to prevent anyone from connecting him back to the secretary of state.

Can observations of a prisoner's actions and mannerisms help to identify him or her?

In fact, Dauger himself wouldn't have had to commit any crime to be imprisoned. He could have had the bad luck to be a butler to an important man, a man who ended up being killed for crimes he had committed against France.

Some experts speculate Dauger may have been imprisoned for what officials thought he knew about his boss. But other historians think Dauger is likely a false name, and no one even knows for sure that he was a butler.

The pretentious prison governor

A much less dramatic theory has more to do with the prison governor than the prisoner. Perhaps there are few records about the Man in the Iron Mask because he really wasn't very important. When his longtime guard, prison governor Saint-Mars, was given this insignificant convict to guard and imprison, Saint-Mars was insulted the man didn't have a higher profile. After all, Saint-Mars felt he himself was a top-ranking official. The stuck-up governor decided to pretend the prisoner was of vital importance.

Saint-Mars's bosses would have known about his pretensions, but would they really have allowed this deception? It seems unlikely there would be no record of it anywhere. Historians know that Saint-Mars was a snob and had a very good opinion of himself. After all, he'd been used to guarding high-level prisoners.

Some people believe it was Saint-Mars who chose to mask the prisoner, to make people wonder who the convict was and assume

he must be of royal birth. That would make the prisoner's jailer, Saint-Mars, seem important, too. Did Saint-Mars build up a centuries-old puzzle just because he was snobby?

The Verdict: Behind the Mask

It's easy to deduce that the prisoner always had to be masked because his face was extremely recognizable. He must have looked so much like someone important that this resemblance would give away his identity at a single glance.

There are no photographs of the Man in the Iron Mask. Photography wasn't invented until more than 100 years after he died. Of course, there was no Internet or television to circulate images of him or anyone else in the 1600s. Even newspapers were still in the early part of their history and didn't include many drawings or sketches.

Who did the Man in the Iron Mask look like that everyone would instantly recognize? Using deductive reasoning, investigators can make a good guess. There was only one face everyone in France in the 1600s knew. It was the face they saw in portraits and on the coins they used daily: the face of their king, Louis XIV.

An uncanny likeness to the king is the most probable reason why the prisoner had to stay masked. Historians speculate the Man in the Iron Mask must have looked enough like the king that he would immediately have been identified as a member of the royal family with just one glimpse. And only the king had the power to imprison his look-alike for most of the poor man's life.

This resemblance meant that the Man in the Iron Mask was likely either the king's secret father or his brother. Perhaps the father knew Louis XIV was his son, and he returned to France looking to exchange his continued silence for more money. Or it's possible the king did have a twin who discovered his real identity when he was an adult and threatened to tell the world, so he had to be imprisoned.

Will the mystery of the Man in the Iron Mask ever be solved? It's possible that ancient, long-forgotten royal records that reveal who he was may still be found. Or perhaps other evidence will be dug up where the Bastille once hid many dark secrets, and historians will use deductive reasoning to identify this legendary prisoner.

But it's unlikely any more facts will turn up for detectives to use to solve this mystery. In 1669, the Man in the Iron Mask dropped out of real life and into myth to create a mystery that's fascinated people for more than three centuries.

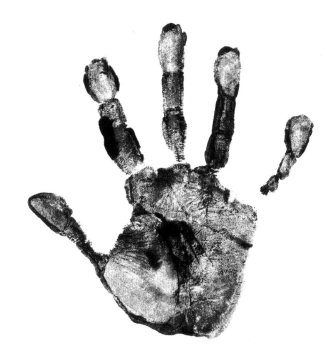

MURDER, ACCIDENT, OR SUICIDE?

The Puzzling Death of Thailand's King Rama VIII

CRIME SCENE

June 9, 1946, Bangkok, Thailand

Crime-Solvers' Arsenal: The Crime Scene

The scene of a crime can tell a vital story. More than 100 years ago, police didn't realize how vital it was to preserve a crime scene. They walked through the area, handling evidence or accidentally removing clues.

Crime scene forensics didn't develop as a science until the 1890s. Today, detectives know the importance of cordoning off the place where a crime has been committed and carefully investigating everything there.

Collecting evidence at a crime scene is a slow and tedious process, but it can solve many mysteries. Although perhaps not all of them …

The Mystery: A Shocking Verdict

"Guilty!"

The courtroom erupted with a bewildered buzz. Guilty? How was that possible? Did the court really mean all three men were responsible for killing their monarch, King Rama VIII of Thailand?

In February 1955, the trio was shot for the crime. After three trials and almost nine years since the king had died, the mystery of who killed Thailand's king was finally solved.

Or was it?

After all, there was one big problem: almost no one believed these men had actually killed the king …

The History: Just the Facts

Sunday, June 9, 1946, dawned sunny and warm. Boromphiman Hall, where Thailand's handsome, 20-year-old king lived, gleamed in the pale morning light. Dragons and other intricately designed creatures decorated the roof and eaves. Golden pinnacles pointed to the sky. The massive doors were encrusted with pearls, and sculptures of strange animals and frightening giants dotted the hallways.

Outside the palace, everything was bright and fair. However, inside, there was a feeling of dark clouds gathering. Ananda, as his family called the king (pronounced *Ananta*), wasn't feeling well. The evening before, the royal physician had diagnosed the slim monarch with indigestion and said he'd soon be fine.

But Ananda's mother, called the Princess Mother, had worked as a nurse, and she worried about him. At about 6:00 the next morning, she visited her son in his wing of the palace, Boromphiman Hall, on the far side from her rooms. Despite being king, Ananda's rooms were plain and simple, and he wore just a light T-shirt and silk pants to bed. The Princess Mother awoke the king, gave him the medicine the doctor had prescribed, and then left to allow Ananda to go back to sleep.

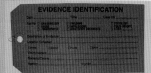

The palace where Ananda lived gleams with gold and precious stones. The palace complex includes the Temple of the Emerald Buddha. But all this wealth and splendor was not enough to save the young king's life.

Shortly after, Butr, one of Ananda's two special pages, or servants, entered the king's dressing room, which was right beside the royal bedroom. Butr had to be at his post the instant the monarch awoke. He waited quietly, ready with the king's glass of orange juice and the day's newspapers.

At about 8:30 a.m., Ananda got up but soon was back in bed, the mosquito net pulled around his bed. He didn't speak to Butr, but simply waved him away. The servant remained waiting in the hall by the dressing room.

Then Nai Chit, Ananda's other page, arrived. Now *that* was strange. Butr and Nai Chit alternated duties and never worked together. But Nai Chit said he was there to take some measurements for a box on behalf of a jeweler he'd just met with. The craftsman was making it for some of the royal family's medals.

Since the medals were kept in a safe in the king's dressing room, Nai Chit decided to wait until the king was awake to get the measurements. The two pages sat together by the dressing room.

Around 9:00 a.m., the king's younger brother, Prince Bhumibol, checked with the pages to see how Ananda was feeling. On hearing the king was still in bed, the prince returned to his room in the opposite wing. Once again, the pages sat down to wait. Then—

BANG!

The peace of the sleepy morning was suddenly shattered. Butr and Nai Chit looked at each other in horror. A pistol shot! And it came from the king's bedroom. Nai Chit raced to the hall's other wing and burst into the Princess Mother's room. "The king's shot himself!" he screamed.

What does the position of a gun in relation to a body say about a crime?

The Princess Mother ran into Ananda's bedroom. There lay her son, stretched out faceup on his bed. Close by Ananda's left hand was a Colt .45 pistol. And on his forehead was a bloody wound.

Nai Chit tore open the mosquito net. The Princess Mother flung herself on her son's body, sobbing. That's where the royal nanny found her a few moments later. When the nanny saw the gun lying on the bed, she feared someone else might get hurt by it. She carefully put it on the bedside cabinet, right beside the glasses Ananda would never wear again.

When Butr later saw the pistol there, he worried that the Princess Mother was distraught and might use it on herself. He took the gun and placed it in a drawer in the dressing room.

Prince Bhumibol arrived next in his brother's bedroom and ordered Butr to call a doctor. He watched helplessly as his mother and the royal nanny tried desperately to stop his brother's bleeding.

The royal physician soon arrived but quickly realized it was too late for him to do anything. The king was dead. Her voice breaking in grief, Ananda's mother asked the doctor to stay to help her clean the body. Since she'd been a nurse, she knew what had to be done. Servants brought in fresh sheets and clothes. Blocks of ice

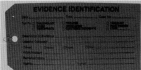
EVIDENCE IDENTIFICATION

King Rama VIII (left) with his mother and his younger brother, Prince Bhumibol, in 1945, the year before Rama died. Did Bhumibol and perhaps even their mother feel Bhumibol would be a better king than Ananda?

were placed down both sides of the bed, and a fan blew over the slim corpse to keep it cool in the tropical heat.

The police chief and his detectives arrived, and began to investigate the crime scene and the king's body. But the chief was stopped immediately. No one must touch royalty! That was a sacred law in Thailand. The police had to be content with just examining the bedroom and questioning the servants and guards.

The police chief could only shake his head in frustration. Hidden in the hopeless jumble of fingerprints, footprints, rumpled sheets, and mess lay the truth about what had happened to the king. The chief would have to bring order to this chaos.

MURDER, ACCIDENT, OR SUICIDE?   65

FINGER-PRINTS

Of course, fingerprints are important clues at any crime scene. Fingerprints were first used to solve a crime in 1892, when Juan Vucetich, an Argentinean police officer, used a bloody thumbprint to link a woman to the murder of her two sons.

Today, detectives use powder and fine brushes to make prints more visible, and then photograph them. Some prints can be lifted off a surface using clear adhesive tape. Then the prints can be compared to those on record for known criminals.

IT'S IN THE BLOOD

Blood can be an important piece of evidence from crime scenes. First of all, police have to determine whether it's human blood or that of another animal. If it belongs to a human, they can test to see which blood group it belongs to. There are four main ones: A, B, O, and AB. This test may determine whether the blood belongs to the criminal, the victim, or someone else.

Careful analysis of blood can show whether a person died of poisoning, suffocation, or other causes. The blood-stains themselves have a story to tell. From the pattern and dispersion of a blood splatter, a detective can figure out how far the blood flew or fell, and the direction it came from.

Blood smears may show the victim was moved after being injured. Bloody fingerprints and shoe prints can give a lot of information about who was at the scene of the crime.

The Clues: The Scene of the Crime

The first thing police want to do when they are called to a crime scene is to block it off so no one can change it in any way before the investigators photograph and examine it. They don't want people walking on important footprints or other evidence. It's also important to prevent any evidence from being moved or removed, accidentally or on purpose.

Detectives usually photograph the crime scene from every angle to make sure they don't miss any evidence. Often, they place a measuring tape in the photos to make lengths and widths clear to anyone examining the photos. An artist may even sketch the scene if the detective thinks the camera won't accurately show an important detail because of lighting, shadows, or placement. And all the while, the detectives take careful notes that not only help them analyze what they see, but also provide evidence they can use in court.

After the scene has been photographed, the search begins. The detectives don't want to contaminate the site with their own shedding skin, hair, or lint. Before they begin, they pull on gloves and cleanroom suits (also called bunny suits), which look like long-sleeved, hooded coveralls that completely cover their clothes. The cleanroom suits also prevent the investigators from carrying away traces of any evidence from the scene.

The police search the scene, sometimes on their hands and knees, moving in a spiral or grid pattern to make sure they inspect everywhere but don't waste time examining the same place twice. Often, they don't even know what they're looking for, and anything can be considered evidence. The detectives may find more weapons, the victim's or suspect's belongings, or more. Even something as small as lint may be evidence of someone having been on the site who left no other trace.

Anything the detectives remove from the scene is placed in a sealed container, to prevent it from being contaminated, and labeled. If anyone tampers with the evidence, it's immediately obvious.

THE TALES BULLETS TELL

When a crime involves guns, police call in ballistics experts. These are scientists who study the motion of bullets, bombs, and other ammunition. The first thing they do at the crime scene is make sure any guns found there can't be fired again. That ensures no one else is hurt.

Then they search for the bullets involved in the crime. These bullets can tell them a lot. First, they have marks on them like fingerprints. They match only one gun, which means the bullets can identify the murder weapon. Investigators also look for any cartridges, the cases around bullets. Most guns and rifles automatically eject cartridges to one side. A criminal rarely thinks to grab them or has time, but cartridges can give a lot of information about the gun that shot them.

By examining where bullets end up, investigators can work out where the gun was when it was fired, and the paths, or trajectories, of the bullets. The direction a bullet travels can reveal whether the shooter was right- or left-handed. The bullet's track may also show that the gun was too far from the body for the victim to have shot himself or if it was at an angle that rules out suicide.

Ballistics experts also analyze gunshot residue (GSR), which is tiny particles—some burned, some not—from the bullet, cartridge, and gun. Experts can learn a lot about the weapon from the metals found in the GSR.

Back in the bedroom

It was almost useless for the police to search Ananda's bedroom after his death. Many people had already been in and out of the room, and evidence—including the king's body—had been moved and even wiped and cleaned! It's not hard to imagine the police chief's frustration when he arrived on the scene.

The pistol found by the king's body had been touched by two people. Who knew who else had touched it and left fingerprints? And the chief wasn't even allowed to touch the king. Neither he nor his detectives could examine the body, not even the bullet wound. There was little point in photographing or sketching anything.

As well, the people the police questioned had had plenty of time not only to come up with stories to emphasize their innocence but also to make sure their tales matched any evidence the other people gave. The bedroom had already been cleaned, which meant any blood splatters had been wiped away. Bloodstain evidence that might have identified a killer was already gone, and there was nothing the chief could do about it.

The chief then asked for the pistol, and the king's servant Nai Chit handed over the gun Butr had put in the drawer. Nai Chit also produced a used cartridge he said he'd found on the floor by Ananda's bed. When the police examined the gun they found it was ready to be fired and was fully loaded—except for just one missing round.

The pillows the king was lying on wouldn't yield any definite evidence since they'd already been moved by his mother and the staff. Days after the death, a blood-covered pillow was found outside in the courtyard. Did it have anything to do with the crime? It was hard for the police to know.

The Speculation: Murder, Accident, or Suicide?

The crime scene in Ananda's bedroom offered little for the police to go on, the eyewitnesses were unreliable, and examining the likely murder weapon wouldn't tell the detectives much. All the police could do was work with the scant evidence they had.

Tragic suicide?

First, they considered the possibility of suicide. Ananda had been ill for a few days, and perhaps he'd been feeling especially depressed that Sunday morning. Perhaps being king was harder than he'd thought. Competing political groups were battling for power in Thailand. Some even wanted to get rid of the royal family completely. How could one inexperienced young man try to rule them all? It must have seemed overwhelming at times.

Then there was the matter of Ananda's love life. In 1943, Ananda had begun studying law in Switzerland. There, he'd fallen in love with one of his classmates, Marylene Ferrari. When his mother discovered the love affair, she'd made it clear to Ananda that as king he would have to marry a Thai woman. The king agreed to break up with Marylene. The Princess Mother had even spoken to the young woman to tell her she had no future with Ananda.

But secretly, the pair had continued to see each other. They also exchanged letters once he was back in Thailand. Lately, the Princess Mother had been pressuring Ananda to choose a Thai wife. How could he give up Marylene? He was barely more than a teenager, and his heart was broken. Was his despair over losing his love enough to drive him to suicide?

The police carefully considered the possibility of suicide. But first, everyone knew what a slight man Ananda was, and his recent illness had made him weaker. The Colt .45 is a very heavy pistol with a strong recoil when it's fired. The king had had trouble controlling it in the past. Would the sick young man have been able to aim it accurately?

Second, Ananda was extremely shortsighted and could do almost nothing without his glasses. Yet they were neatly folded on his bedside cabinet, not on his face. It's unlikely he could have made the gun ready to fire without wearing his glasses.

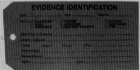
Ananda loved shooting automatic guns. Here he is at a camp near Bangkok, inspecting soldiers and firing a Colt .45 automatic pistol. This was the gun discovered by his side when his mother found his body.

Last, the pistol was found by the king's left hand, but Ananda was right-handed, although he *could* have used both hands.

Accident?

Or was Ananda's death a tragic accident? The pistol was one of his favorite guns, and he had always kept it by his bedside. Maybe he had been handling the gun carelessly because he was ill, and it had gone off in his hands. Perhaps accidental death was the solution to this crime investigation. But the police considered this unlikely for all the same reasons they'd ruled out suicide.

Brotherly mistake?

What if Bhumibol had accidently shot his brother? It was certainly possible. The king and his brother were close. They looked alike,

both of them slim and dark with glasses, although Bhumibol was two years younger than the king, was shorter, and had a wider face.

The brothers also had similar interests. Both young men liked to fire off guns, and they often spent time together with their collection of firearms. Prince Bhumibol even thought it was fun to point a pistol at his kingly brother and pretend to fire it. Not surprisingly, the king didn't find this nearly as amusing as the prince did.

On that fateful morning, had Bhumibol aimed the gun at his ill brother, trying to distract him and make him forget his sickness? Then perhaps his warped joke went one step too far when he accidentally fired the gun, with deadly results.

Murder: motive, motive, who's got a motive?

If the police decided the king had been murdered, they didn't have to look far for possible suspects. For a young man, Ananda had a lot of enemies.

His pages had worked for the royal family for a long time, but their behavior on the morning he died was very odd. It was unusual that Nai Chit had shown up in the king's rooms hours before his daily shift would start. He said he was there to measure some medals to allow a jeweler to make a case for them. But had Nai Chit really met with a jeweler before 9:00 on a Sunday morning, as he claimed?

Then there was Nai Chit's telltale call for help. After all, it wasn't clear Nai Chit had even been in Ananda's bedroom before he ran to the Princess Mother yelling, "The king's shot himself!" How did he know the king had committed suicide? Did he yell this to stop people from looking for a murderer? Although Nai Chit would have known the king would not be alone because Butr was on duty, perhaps he had hoped Butr would be off running an errand, giving him an opportunity for murder.

The king may also have been murdered by scheming politicians who thought they'd prefer Bhumibol on the throne. He was younger than his brother and still a teenager. They might have assumed they could push him around more easily. They might also

FROM SIAM TO THAILAND

In 1939, when King Rama VIII was just 14 years old, he changed the name of his country from Siam to Thailand. In the Thai language, Siam means "dark" and has a negative meaning. But, according to some experts, Thai means "freedom."

DEATH FORETOLD?

Just two months before the king's death, one of his staff had a premonition and insisted on trading places with the king in a motorcade. A few minutes later, the man was killed when a rockslide hit his car, the one in which the king had just been riding.

have believed they could scare the new king: if he didn't do what they wanted, he would meet the same fate as his poor, dead brother. Bhumibol might have feared for his own life, and what the effect of losing two sons would have on his devastated mother.

Other people had reasons to kill Ananda. There were many warring groups in Thailand who all wanted power. Some thought they could achieve this best without a king; others wanted to control the king. If one group could assassinate their monarch and then throw the blame on another, that was even better.

The police also had to consider the possibility of bribery. Perhaps the king's pages had been promised money by one of Thailand's political groups to keep silent about anything they saw that morning. After all, since about 7:00 a.m., Butr had been on duty outside the king's bedroom. No murderer had slipped past him to commit the tragic crime. At least, that's what Butr said. Perhaps Butr and Nai Chit had been paid to allow an assassin into the king's rooms. If that was the case, the murderer could have been almost anyone.

Even Prince Bhumibol had his reasons to kill the king. After all, with Ananda's death, Bhumibol became king. Not only would he no longer be just an unimportant little brother, he would also have supreme power and amazing wealth. Had he somehow slipped into his brother's bedroom when the servants weren't looking and shot the sleeping king? Even if the staff had discovered his crime, it would be easy for the new king to pay them to keep silent. The younger brother knew where the king kept the pistol, and he knew how to use it. Bhumibol had a good motive for murder, and the opportunity to commit it.

But despite the speculation, it was hard to really picture Bhumibol as his brother's murderer. He was nowhere near the king's bedroom when the gunshot rang out. Besides, he genuinely loved his brother. After the king's death, it was a very long time before Bhumibol smiled again, let alone laughed. The prince also must have seen how his brother had struggled with the difficulties

Ananda (left) and his brother, Prince Bhumibol, seemed to be the best of friends, but were they? Or was Bhumibol jealous enough of his older brother's power and wealth to kill him?

of being Thailand's king. Would he really have wanted to take on these problems for himself?

If Bhumibol *had* killed his brother, it is possible that the Princess Mother could have been part of the plot. If she had suspected her younger son was the killer, she might have tried to cover up for him rather than lose both her boys. By throwing herself on the king's body, and then later asking the doctor to help her clean her son, she destroyed vital evidence. Did she do this unthinkingly, trying to occupy herself to lessen her grief a little? Or was she making sure there were no traces connecting the murder to Bhumibol or someone else? No one knew why she did it, but the tidying made it impossible for police to reconstruct the crime scene.

Why might even the king's mother be a suspect?

Even Ananda's mother had her own motives for killing her son, the police had heard. It was well known she favored her younger son and found him easier to control than his older brother. Did she prefer Bhumibol enough to murder Ananda, give the younger man the throne, and become the power behind that throne?

It was almost impossible for the police to pin the murder on any of the suspects. None of them seemed more guilty than the others. Perhaps the king had been assassinated, but the police couldn't say who committed the crime.

Then there was one more problem: the Colt .45 as the murder weapon. When experts examined the pistol, they determined it hadn't been shot in at least a week. The real murder weapon must have been carried away, likely by the murderer.

Why did Thailand's king die?

The court rules

In October 1946, the commission investigating the king's death ruled it couldn't have been accidental. However, the officials also said the evidence didn't prove suicide or murder. But that was just the beginning. In November 1947, Butr and Nai Chit, the king's two servants, and Senator Chaleo Patoomros were arrested for the murder.

Chaleo was a former personal secretary to the king but was now associated with Pridi Banmyong, Thailand's premier. Pridi had once tried to overthrow the country's monarchy, and now many thought he'd either killed the king or arranged the assassination. Perhaps Chaleo was the killer, but he had not been seen at the palace that morning, and most people thought he'd been framed.

The trial of Butr, Nai Chit, and Chaleo started in August 1948 and finally ended in May 1951. During this time, the three men's lawyers resigned and were replaced, only to have two of the new lawyers arrested and charged with treason. Another lawyer then resigned, leaving just one young lawyer.

The court found that the king had been assassinated and Nai Chit had somehow been involved. However, the murder charges against Butr and Chaleo were dismissed, and they were released.

But the strange story of Ananda's death wasn't over yet. Nai Chit appealed the verdict. More than a year later, another court again found him guilty. Not only that, but they decided Butr was guilty after all. Not surprisingly, Butr and Nai Chit took their case to Thailand's Supreme Court. Deliberations continued for 10 months. And yet again, the court's decision shocked everyone: the two men were again found guilty, and this time Chaleo was also found guilty.

The three men were imprisoned. Then, secretly and without warning, they were executed in February 1955.

The Verdict: Thailand's Uneasy King

Today, many people in Thailand believe that Butr, Nai Chit, and Chaleo were innocent. But still no one knows how Ananda died or who killed him. Ananda's death and Bhumibol's throne are shrouded in a web of intrigue. Some people say Bhumibol is controlled by his enemies and that they continue to hold power over him by keeping alive the rumor that he killed his brother.

There's one big reason why the cause of Ananda's death is still a mystery more than 60 years later. No one in Thailand is allowed to talk about the king's death or say anything against the royal family. People who dare to can be arrested. Ananda's death changed the country's history, but it's not even taught in schools.

Today, Bhumibol, or King Rama IX, is the richest royal in the world, worth more than $30 billion. But immediately after his brother's death, this cheerful, happy boy became a grief-stricken young man known for never smiling. No one's certain if his sadness is because he misses his brother—or because he regrets killing him.

There are experts who think Bhumibol may know a lot more than he's saying. He's now a very old man. Some people hope that when he dies, he will leave behind a full explanation of his brother's death. Perhaps then the mystery of King Rama VIII's death will finally be solved.

RUSSIAN RIDDLE

Did Grand Duchess Anastasia Survive a Royal Massacre?

CRIME SCENE

July 17, 1918, Ekaterinburg, Russia

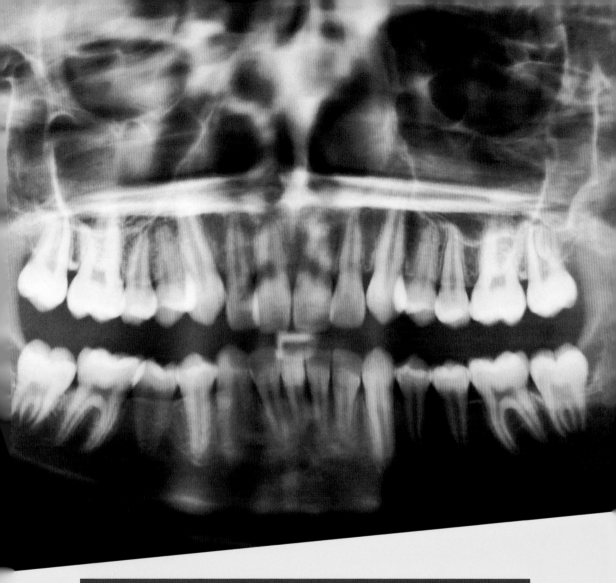

Crime-Solvers' Arsenal: Establishing Identity

Today, DNA can help confirm a person's identity beyond a reasonable doubt, but this exact science is recent. How did detectives solve crimes before they could use such tools as DNA matching (page 136) or CT scans (page 114)?

Well, since the late 1800s, investigators have relied on such techniques as fingerprinting, dental records, or handwriting analysis. And when royal wealth and power are at risk, detectives are forced to use any means they can.

The Mystery: Grand Duchess or Imposter?

"Silence! Silence in the court!"

It was the moment people had been anticipating for decades. When this trial had started in 1938, the woman at the center of it was just 42 years old. Now, in 1970, Anna Anderson was a frail old lady of 73. The judge was about to rule on whether or not she was really Grand Duchess Anastasia Nikolaevna of Russia, only survivor of that country's murdered royal family.

This was the longest trial in German history. It was held in Germany because that's where Anna was living when the trial started. Lawyers presented hundreds of witnesses and thousands of pages of testimony. Arguments had been heated, and the outcome was uncertain.

At stake was ownership of the riches of the dead Romanov family, believed to be in the millions of dollars. Anna Anderson's opponents in the case were mostly relatives of the family, who were in line to inherit this wealth. But first, they had to prove Anna was not a grand duchess but a factory worker named Franziska Schanzkowska. Also at stake was the wish for a happy ending to the horrific story of the Russian royal family's execution.

The crowd fell silent as the judge prepared to speak. Would he decide that Anna Anderson was Anastasia? Or would he denounce her as a fraud? Finally, he pronounced his verdict about Anna's identity: "Neither established nor refuted."

While Anna had not been found to be Anastasia, neither had she been declared an imposter. And the mystery of Anastasia and Anna Anderson continued …

The History, Part 1: Life as a Grand Duchess

Anastasia sighed. Life was very different now that her father was no longer emperor of Russia. Since her family had been brought to Ekaterinburg, not only was it not fun, but it was also frightening.

Anastasia was about 13 when this photo was taken of her with her family. From left to right, they are her sister Olga, her sister Marie, her father, her mother, Anastasia, her brother, Alexei, and her sister Tatiana.

The little princess thought back to her family's home in Petrograd (now St. Petersburg), the country's capital. It covered three city blocks, and everywhere inside was marble, gilt, sparkling chandeliers, luxurious chairs, and brocade-covered sofas. They only stayed there in the winter. In the summer, they spent the days sailing on their yacht.

Anastasia laughed and joked all the time back then, and instead of studying like she was supposed to, she spent much of her time thinking up new mischief. Sometimes she drove her older sisters Olga, Tatiana, and Maria crazy with her pranks. She also knew just how to tease her little brother, Alexei, but when she did, her mother, Czarina Alexandra, would scold her. Anastasia always had lots of energy, despite her painful bunions, which caused large bumps at the base of her big toes and sometimes made walking very difficult for her.

EVIDENCE IDENTIFICATION

A section of the beautiful Catherine Palace, just one of the lavish homes that belonged to Anastasia's family. No wonder people hoped Anastasia had survived her family's massacre and might share her wealth with supporters.

What Anastasia probably didn't know was that her father, Czar Nikolay, wasn't a strong emperor. He found it hard to make necessary decisions. His father had died unexpectedly, and Nikolay had received little training on ruling the huge country of Russia. At the time, Russia covered more than one-sixth of the earth's land, the largest empire on the planet.

Maybe even a strong emperor wouldn't have made a difference. Royalty was losing its power in Russia as the country moved toward revolution. The common people were angry with the laws that Nikolay imposed and that kept them impoverished.

Russian revolutionaries

When World War I began in 1914, Russians fought bravely for their country and at first had many victories. This was despite the fact that they often had no shoes, no ammunition, and no weapons. By 1916, more than 1.5 million Russian soldiers had died, and twice as many were missing or were prisoners of war. Many Russians blamed their czar and his poor leadership.

Anastasia was just 15 in February 1917 when riots broke out in Petrograd. By March 2, the Russian government forced the czar to abdicate, or give up his throne. "Good-bye," Anastasia wrote to a friend. "Don't forget us."

The little princess and her family were held prisoner at Alexander Palace, near Petrograd. Soldiers yelled at them and mocked them. When their guards gave them permission, the family could walk outside, but that was almost worse. The crowds at the gates shouted insults at them.

What might the soldiers' actions say about how the prisoners will be treated later?

More and more Russians were siding with the revolutionaries. They believed in socialism, a system for producing and sharing goods, including food, fairly. No wonder starving peasants supported it. It would mean an end to a system where a handful of people had untold wealth while others couldn't house, clothe, or even feed their families.

The Bolsheviks, a large organization of revolutionaries, were anti-royalty, and the Russian government became worried that the Romanovs could be hurt—or worse. In August 1917, the family was sent to Tobolsk, Siberia, far from the violence of the revolution.

Red October

Two months later, the Bolsheviks seized power in a revolution that became known as Red October. The royal family became terrified of what might lie ahead for them. They made plans to leave their

By the winter of 1917, Anastasia (second from right) and her family were in captivity in Tobolsk. No longer dressed in jewels and expensive clothes, her sister Olga (left), her father, and her sister Tatiana were happy just to be together.

beloved country and go somewhere where they'd be safe. Then, in April 1918, the Bolsheviks ordered Nikolay to leave Tobolsk. His wife, Alexandra, and their daughter Maria went with him, although none of them knew where they were going.

Anastasia, her sisters Olga and Tatiana, and her little brother, Alexei, were scared. Anxiously, they waited for a letter from their parents. Czarina Alexandra soon wrote that they'd been sent to Ekaterinburg in southeastern Russia. And she also gave her daughters a coded message telling them to "dispose of the medicines."

The girls knew what that meant. They were to hide their precious jewels and gems by sewing them into the hems of their skirts, hats, jackets, and even corsets. Historians later estimated the girls had about 8 kilograms (18 pounds) of jewels sewn into their clothes.

Then they were all summoned to Ekaterinburg. By May 1918, the royals were together again.

Any relief they felt at being reunited was short-lived. Conditions in Ekaterinburg were terrible. In the house where they were held prisoner, the windows were whitewashed to prevent the family from seeing out. Food was scarce: sometimes there was none, or sometimes the only food they had, the Bolshevik guards had spat in.

When Anastasia stuck her head out a window one day, she was shot at. When she asked if she could get a pair of shoes from her luggage, the guard rudely refused. She was told she didn't need them—the shoes she was wearing would last longer than she would. The little princess shivered, but when the guard turned his back on her, cleaning staff noticed she stuck out her tongue at him. Typical Anastasia!

Terror at night

Just after midnight on July 17, 1918, Anastasia and her family were awakened and told to dress because they were being moved to a safer location. The Romanovs were herded down to the basement, where they were told to wait.

Suddenly, Bolshevik soldiers armed with guns and bayonets appeared at the doorway. "Your relatives have tried to save you," one of them announced. "They have failed, and we are obliged to shoot you all."

With that, the soldiers began firing. They killed the czar first, then his wife. But when they shot at the Romanov daughters, the bullets bounced off the girls! The soldiers couldn't believe their eyes! They didn't know about the gems sewn into the girls' clothes. Bullets ricocheted wildly around the room. Finally, the soldiers shot each daughter in the head, or brutally stabbed and clubbed them.

The bodies of the royal family were dumped onto a waiting truck, then driven off into the night. It's thought that the corpses were first dropped into a nearby mine. But the soldiers wanted to keep their deadly deed secret, and the bodies weren't well

Photos like this of Anastasia would later provide important information about the shape of her ears, the size of her mouth, the distance between her nose and eyes, and more.

concealed there. So they moved the bodies to a shallow grave nearby.

The Bolsheviks tried to cover up the massacre by spreading various stories to confuse the Russian people. First, they said only Czar Nikolay had been killed. Then they reported that the rest of the family had fled the country. Rumors sprang up that at least one of the grand duchesses had still been alive when the bodies of the royal family were removed from the house. It wasn't until 1920 that the world was told the entire family had been executed.

Anastasia's name means "resurrection," and it was no surprise that people began to believe that she was the one who had survived the massacre …

The History, Part 2: Miss Unknown

Splash! Sergeant Hallman ran toward the nearby canal. Someone had just fallen—or jumped!—into the murky, frigid water. It was a cold February night in Berlin, Germany, in 1920, and Hallman knew he had to fish out the midnight swimmer quickly.

But when he did, the soaking-wet young woman wasn't at all grateful that he'd foiled her suicide attempt. She refused to admit who she was, saying only that she had her reasons for not speaking. The police named her Fräulein Unbekannt, or Miss Unknown. She seemed crazed with fear, and since no one knew what to do with her, she was placed in an institution for the mentally ill.

When doctors examined her, they were puzzled by the strange scar behind her ear. It looked like a bullet wound. They could tell Miss Unknown had taken a hard hit to the face because her jaw and the bone at the top of her nose had been broken. She was also missing eight teeth, and at least seven more were loose.

A scar on Miss Unknown's foot suggested it had been stabbed with some sort of spike, or even a bayonet. She had many other old wounds and scars. Miss Unknown also had painful bunions on her feet. The patient was usually fairly docile and quiet, but she struggled against having her photo taken. "If people knew who I am, I would not be here," she claimed.

The beginning of the legend

Miss Unknown was still in the institution in fall 1921, when another patient became convinced the young woman was Tatiana, one of Russia's grand duchesses. But when asked if she was Tatiana, Miss Unknown refused to speak.

A few months later, the second patient was released from the institution, and she convinced some people who had known the Romanovs to come and meet "Tatiana." When the former czarina's lady-in-waiting visited, Miss Unknown retreated under her blankets. The lady-in-waiting tore off the blankets and said with disgust,

"She's too short for Tatiana." But after the disastrous visit, Miss Unknown calmly said, "I never said I was Tatiana." She soon admitted to her supporters her real identity: Anastasia.

Miss Unknown made no attempt to befriend or convince supporters or Romanov relatives of her identity. Often, she would hide under her blanket or wouldn't utter a word. But sometimes she would answer questions, and she seemed to know things that only a member of the royal family could know.

Miss Unknown eventually told a story of somehow surviving the massacre that had killed her family, and waking up in a farm cart on a country road. She had no idea how she got there, but she was cared for by a kind family. One of them came with her to Berlin to find her aunt Irene, the czarina's sister.

When Miss Unknown became separated from the fellow she'd traveled with, she panicked. Worried that her aunt would not recognize her, Miss Unknown had decided to commit suicide rather than go on any longer.

No matter what tricks visitors tried, Miss Unknown refused to speak Russian, although she seemed to understand it. Nurses revealed that she seemed to speak it in her sleep. But awake, she refused "because it was the last language we heard in that house." Some people said she spoke English, French, and German, all languages that Anastasia had studied.

Was she or wasn't she?

Soon people began to call her Anna. When she left the institution, she went to live in the home of one of the many supporters who believed she was Anastasia. Perhaps her new friends hoped to be rewarded for their service to the supposed grand duchess. After all, everyone had heard the stories about the vast riches that Czar Nikolay had stashed away outside of Russia. If her supporters could prove that Anna was Anastasia, then perhaps she would show her gratitude by sharing her wealth with them.

But Anna was difficult to live with. Her mood could change

EVIDENCE IDENTIFICATION

The Grand Duchess Olga Alexandrovna was Anastasia's aunt. Olga met Anna in 1925 and for months was one of the many people who were convinced Anna was Anastasia (see page 90). But Olga later changed her mind.

from charming to enraged in moments. She sulked, argued rudely with her hosts about everything from food to flower arrangements, and complained bitterly whenever she felt she was being treated like less than the daughter of an emperor.

Anna was passed from one supporter to another as they grew tired of caring for her and keeping up with her demands. Many people who had known Anastasia came to visit Anna to decide for themselves whether the grand duchess was actually still alive.

These duchesses and princes, and the staff and tutors, all commented on the fact that Anna never tried to coax them to recognize her as Anastasia. She simply acted as if she was Anastasia, and she didn't care if anyone agreed with her. But people did comment on

Anna's similarities to Anastasia. Both had a mark on the shoulder where a mole had been removed, and they had the same painful foot affliction. Could the mark on Anna's foot have come from one of the soldier's bayonets on that fateful night?

Grand Duchess Olga Alexandrovna, Anastasia's favorite aunt, couldn't make up her mind about Anna. "My intelligence will not allow me to accept her as Anastasia," she said, "but my heart tells me that it is she." Most people had a similar reaction. Some were convinced she had to be Anastasia, while others felt she must be an imposter.

Who is Franziska?

Some of the Romanovs' living relatives decided to do their own investigation into Anna's past. In 1927, Czarina Alexandra's brother, Grand Duke Ernest Louis, paid for detectives to inquire into her identity. They discovered that about the same time Anna was saved from the canal in Berlin, a factory worker named Franziska Schanzkowska in the same city went missing.

Franziska was Polish, so she spoke a language similar to Russian. She would have understood Anastasia's main language, but of course would not have been able to speak it as well as the grand duchess had. Did this explain why Anna never spoke Russian?

At first, Franziska's family said they recognized Anna, but then they claimed they weren't sure. They knew that if they identified Anna as Franziska, she would go to jail for being a fraud. Perhaps they pretended not to know her because they didn't want her to be imprisoned. Eventually, most people forgot about Franziska. But they did not forget Anna.

Court case with no verdict

In 1928, Anna moved to the United States. By now, she was quite famous and used the name Anna Anderson to avoid publicity. That's how most people remember her today. She traveled back and forth between Europe and the United States, with friends paying all of her expenses, waiting for the day when she regained her grand duchess title.

Meanwhile, Anna was becoming even more eccentric and impossible to deal with. She threw tantrums, killed her pet parakeet, and ended up spending more time in a mental hospital.

In 1938, Anastasia's relatives began their court case against Anna in Germany, where some of them were living. They wanted access to the Romanov inheritance, which they felt belonged to them. Anna didn't seem to really care about the outcome of the case. She never tried to influence witnesses to have them speak in her favor. Many people took this as an obvious sign that she really was Anastasia. It didn't bother her when the case ended in 1970 with no firm decision. *She* knew who she was.

In 1979, Anna was living in Virginia when she began to have severe stomach problems. At a nearby hospital, a tumor and a length of intestine were removed. Although she recovered from the surgery, her health remained poor, and she died in 1984. Her death certificate listed her father as "Czar Nikolay."

What can mental illness reveal? That a person is covering something up? She's tortured by guilt? Or she's suffering because no one believes her?

The Clues: Face to Face

Today, scientists use DNA to establish people's identity, and eventually this did provide a solution to the mystery surrounding Anastasia and Anna. But DNA is a relatively new technology. When Anna's case was being tried in court, other techniques had to be used to try to prove her identity.

Facial comparison

One method used in Anna's case was to compare her face to photos of Anastasia to see if they matched. In those days, researchers used rulers and grids to help them measure the shape of the eyes, nose, mouth, and ears. They looked at how far apart these features were and their placement on the face. Today, forensic scientists can use computers to calculate these statistics.

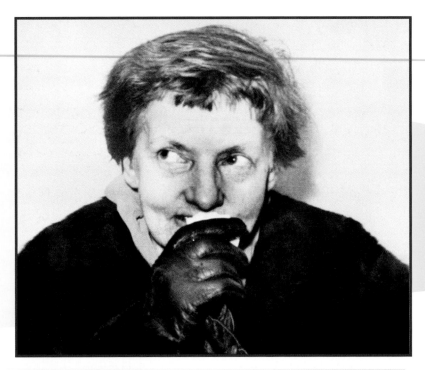

Anna often covered her mouth in photos. Some people thought this was because she was ashamed of her bad teeth. Others said she was hiding how much fuller her lips were than Anastasia's.

Many photos of Anna show her biting her lip. In other photos, you can see her large, full lips. Photos of Anastasia show she had thin lips, and some people argue that Anna was trying to make herself look more like Anastasia. Many people commented on how similar Anna's eyes and the upper part of her face were to Anastasia's. However, Anna often hid the lower part of her face behind a handkerchief or feather boa. Or she pulled up a sheet and hid completely! Her supporters insisted this was because she was ashamed that she had few teeth. But was this really the reason?

Dental records

Some of Anna's detractors claimed that when Anna heard the imperial dentist was going to examine her mouth, she had many teeth pulled, including healthy ones, because she knew her teeth were very different from Anastasia's. It's true that the teeth had been causing her pain, but to many, the timing of the extractions seemed a little suspicious.

Dental records are often still used to identify victims of natural disasters or long-ago crimes who are otherwise not identifiable. It's called odontology, and identifying people by their teeth goes back to ancient Rome. Detectives can also use dental records to identify bite marks because everybody's bite is unique.

Dentists keep X-rays or other records that show the shape and number of teeth, the formation of the jaw, cavities (how many and in which teeth), and more. The teeth of a nameless victim can be examined for all of these things in hopes of making a match and identifying the person.

The imperial dentist carefully compared a cast of Anna's jaw to a plaster impression that had been made of Anastasia's teeth. He quickly decided there were no similarities between them.

All ears

Every pair of ears is different, and these differences can also help detectives identify people. Detectives look at the complicated arches and curls to see if they match exactly. In Anna's case, one expert found that her ear matched Anastasia's in 17 ways, which were more matches than German law required to prove identity.

There was just one hitch: many people were sure the expert was comparing Anna's ear not to Anastasia's ear but to her sister Maria's ear. Some people even said he was comparing a left ear to a right ear, and that the two were different. In the end, the ear similarities didn't prove anything.

Handwriting

A person's handwriting is a useful identification tool because we all write differently. Forensic scientists used handwriting analysis to decide whether Anna Anderson was Anastasia. This kind of analysis is called questioned document examination (QDE), and it may also include determining when a document was created, deciding whether it is counterfeit, or deciphering information on the document that's been erased.

Graphologists (handwriting experts) look not only at the loops and shape of individual letters but also at groups of letters and how they're joined. They examine the size of the letters and where a subject starts writing—for instance, right at the top of the page or over to the right.

At first, Anna and Anastasia's handwriting was judged to be too similar to have been written by different women. But later, the court said there hadn't been enough samples to compare. Nurses at the institution where Anna originally stayed remembered she practiced copying Anastasia's signature. This is known as forging or unnatural writing, in which the writer tries to control or alter her usual style. No wonder there was a match at first.

Fingerprinting

Fingerprint identification, also known as dactyloscopy, is a technique still used extensively by forensic scientists. Everyone has unique fingerprints, and if detectives find a print at a crime scene that matches yours, then there's no doubt that you were there. Even each of your fingers has a slightly different print. Take a look.

Detectives can lift fingerprints from almost any surface. They may apply a special dust to make the prints more obvious. Back at the lab, they feed the fingerprints into a database to see if they already have the prints on file with a criminal's name attached.

Today, live scan fingerprinting makes the process easy. People place their fingertips on a screen, and a scanner creates an electronic image of the fingerprints. The machines are small and portable, and make it faster than ever to compare new prints to the millions already on file.

Despite much searching, no fingerprint of Anastasia's could ever be found. Although Anna's fingerprints had been taken when

AN EYE FOR ANALYSIS

To examine handwriting, a forensic scientist needs excellent eyesight, strong light, and a good magnifier. Today, there are software programs to compare samples of handwriting, but during Anna Anderson's court case, the graphologist had to compare the samples by eye.

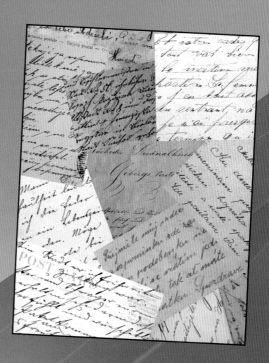

NO PRINTS?

Although clever criminals wear gloves to leave no prints behind, a complete lack of prints can also be a clue to detectives that someone was at a crime scene but was anxious that no one else know. But even smart crooks make mistakes, and forensic scientists know the places where lawbreakers are most likely to slip up and leave their prints.

she was placed in an institution after she was pulled from the canal, there was nothing to compare them to. This was a dead end in her identification.

THE VERDICT: Mystery Finally Solved

Until 1976, no one knew for sure what had happened to the Romanov family or where their bodies had been buried. But almost 60 years after their deaths, amateur Russian historians read notes in a special archive and figured out the site of the royals' burial. However, the political situation in Russia at the time was still very anti-monarchy, and they were scared to come forward with their findings. Instead, they kept silent until 1989, when the communist form of government established by the Bolsheviks after the deaths of the Romanovs was finally overturned in Russia.

The bones speak

Two years after that, the grave was reopened by an amateur historian. But mystery still hung over the fateful night of the Romanov massacre because two of the bodies were missing. DNA testing (page 136) showed that none of the bones belonged to a young boy, which meant Alexei's body must have been one of the missing ones. One of the daughters was also missing, but experts couldn't agree whether the missing girl was Maria—or Anastasia.

Anna Anderson had been cremated when she died in 1984, and people assumed no one could obtain any samples of her DNA to see if it matched the royal family's. Researchers checked at a hospital in Virginia near where Anna had lived at the end of her life, but the hospital wasn't able to turn up any tissue for testing.

Then, months later, someone at the hospital remembered that Anna had had surgery there, and a sample of her intestine had been stored. A sample of her hair also turned up in a book belonging to someone close to her. Suddenly, there was lots of material to check for DNA.

In 1994, the DNA analysis was completed. A comparison of Anna's DNA to that of Romanov relatives showed absolutely no similarity. But that wasn't the only testing that was done. Anna's DNA was also compared to DNA of relatives of Franziska Schanzkowska (page 90). And there was most certainly a match.

You might think that would make Anna Anderson's supporters give up. Not at all. They claimed it was suspicious that the hospital had first said they had no samples of Anna's tissue and then suddenly came up with some. And the hair samples had been found in an envelope with Anna's name on it, but did that really mean it was Anna's?

Anna's supporters also suggested DNA had been switched or contaminated, and that the scientists doing the testing had been paid to provide a certain result. After all, Anastasia's body had still not definitely been found. Her supporters felt it was still possible that Anna really was Anastasia.

Then, in 2007, near the large burial site, researchers found a small grave containing the bones of two teenagers, a boy and a girl. More DNA testing proved that finally all of the doomed Romanovs had been found. It wasn't clear whether Anastasia had been buried in the big grave or the little one, but it was obvious that she had not survived the Romanov massacre. At last the world knew what had happened to her, and that Anna Anderson had never been Anastasia.

"In no any way whatsoever"

People wanted to believe Anastasia had survived the brutal massacre. The years leading up to the 1918 execution had been filled with such devastating events as the sinking of the *Titanic* (1912), World War I (1914–1918), the Bolshevik revolution (1917), and more. People around the world wished to believe that a young girl had outsmarted armed soldiers and miraculously survived execution.

It's strange that Anastasia went from being the youngest, most insignificant of the Russian princesses to the most famous. Books, movies, plays, and even a ballet have been created about her.

DNA testing can show who someone isn't. How can you then prove the person's real identity?

THE TRUTH BEHIND THE FACTS

How did Anna know a lot about the royal family, things that only a real insider would know, such as the names of pets, where certain rooms were in their palace, and events from Anastasia's childhood? Some people say that she was told special facts by Romanov relatives or staff who perhaps hoped to be rewarded when Anna was given the Romanov fortune. Others suggest that people asked her questions such as, "You remember your special nickname was Shvipsik, don't you?" and therefore gave away the answer in the question. (*Shvipsik* is Russian for "imp"!)

It seemed that people heard what they wanted to hear and believed what they wanted to believe about Anna. Or perhaps maybe the promise of money changed their minds.

If the judge had ruled that Anna was Anastasia, she would have owned beautiful jewelry like this.

Former United States president John F. Kennedy once said that Anastasia's story was the only part of Russian history that really interested him!

Even more famous than Anastasia and the entire Russian royal family was factory worker Franziska Schanzkowska, who became known around the world as Anna Anderson. Everyone who met her, even those determined to expose her as a fraud, said there was something special about her. Although the puzzle of her identity has been solved, it's still a mystery how she could keep people guessing for such a long time.

And the mystery of the fortune that everyone seemed sure Nikolay had deposited in banks outside Russia, the riches that started that decades-long court case? There are records suggesting that, during World War I, the czar took his money out of the international banks to bring it back to Russia to help the economy. It was all lost during the revolution. Nothing has ever been found: no fabulous jewels, no gold, no money.

This is one longtime royal mystery that modern technology solved when years of research couldn't find an answer. But if Anna Anderson were still alive, she wouldn't have cared. "You either believe it or you don't believe it," said Anna. "It doesn't matter. In no any way whatsoever."

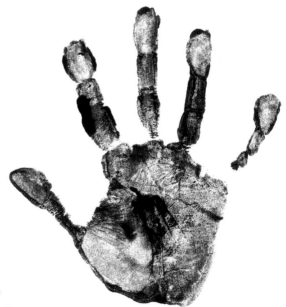

MYSTERIOUS EGYPTIAN ENDING

How Did King Tut Die?

CRIME SCENE

1323 BCE, Valley of the Kings, Egypt

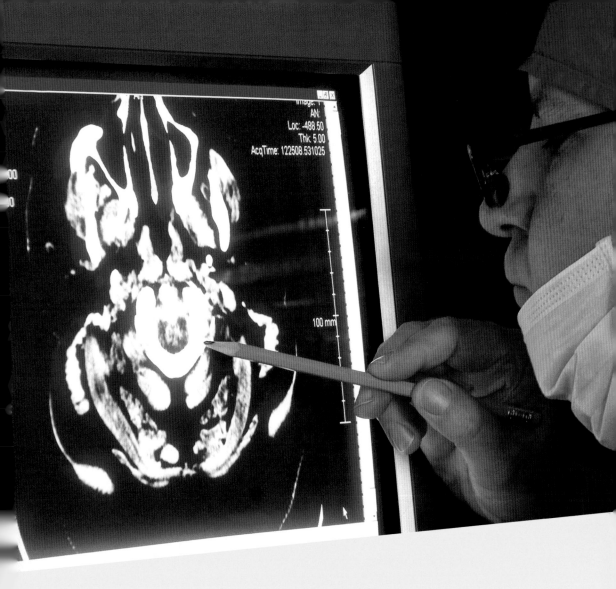

Image: 1
AN:
Loc: -488.50
Thk: 5.00
AcqTime: 122508.531025

100 mm

Crime-Solvers' Arsenal: Medical Imagery (CT Scans)

Since 1974, CT scans have given doctors lots of useful information about diseases in living people. These specialized X-rays show both a patient's soft tissue and bones.

Forensic detectives also use CT scans in their search for clues about how a person died. These scans may answer questions about people who have been dead for many years. CT scans can even help solve mysteries involving ancient mummies.

The Mystery: A Fateful Chariot Ride

Oh! The pain! Tut stood up slowly, putting all his weight on his walking stick. The throbbing in his feet was getting worse. What agony! How long before he wouldn't be able to stand at all? Already, he had to sit to shoot arrows when he was hunting.

Ever since he'd been king, Tut had this excruciating pain, despite the best efforts of his royal doctors. And on top of the pain, the young king had many things on his mind. Tut decided to go for a chariot ride, perhaps to put his troubles behind him. He loved hunting wild animals and was a good shot with his bow and arrow. How could he have guessed that it would be his last chariot ride?

The History, Part 1: A King Too Young?

King Tutankhamun (pronounced *Toot-ahnk-ah-MOON*) was only 19, far too young to have such aches and pains. The short, slim young man had been Egypt's ruler for 10 years. And what a difficult rule it had been, especially at the beginning. When his father, Akhenaton, had died, he'd left a kingdom in chaos. The old king had ignored his country to pursue a new religion, while his staff and even other countries took advantage of his neglect.

Restoring Egypt's power and importance was one of Tut's main aims as king. He relied heavily on his prime minister, Ay, who was about 20 years older and much more experienced. Ay had taught the young king everything he knew about negotiation, diplomacy, governing—and political intrigue. Sometimes Tut thought Ay would make a better king.

Though Tut was head of Egypt's army, he knew that Horemheb, the commander-in-chief of the country's forces, was far more knowledgeable in military campaigns. It bothered the teenager that he depended heavily on these men. And Tut knew that his wife was unhappy, too. Ankhesenamen desperately wanted to have children, but the couple had none.

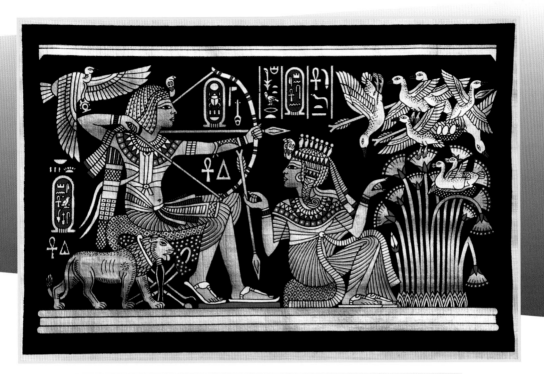

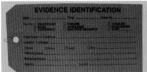
This image, which dates to about 1300 BCE, shows King Tut sitting down to shoot arrows. Experts believe standing was too painful for the young king. But what caused this pain?

As Tut raced out over the dunes in his chariot that fateful day, he scanned the desert for deer, ostriches, and leopards. Even a rabbit would do. He didn't see the crack in one of his chariot wheels growing bigger and bigger. Suddenly, the wheel snapped. The chariot teetered, then flipped over, landing on top of the young king, while the horses neighed and struggled against their harnesses.

The pain was worse than anything Tut had ever experienced. He looked down at his throbbing left leg and saw to his horror that his thigh bone had broken and pierced his skin. Tut didn't have long to live. The break became infected, and his weakened body couldn't fight the infection off. In 1323 BCE, Tut died.

Word spread quickly that King Tut was dead. Intrigue and murder were not unusual among Egyptian royals, but Tut was

young and hadn't made many enemies yet. His tumble from the chariot could have been an accident. However, the rumors quickly began that he may have been murdered. Why had his chariot flipped? Some people wondered if it had been sabotaged. Others wondered why anyone would want him dead.

Death of a king

Tut was young and his death unexpected, so his royal tomb was not yet ready for him. The builders had assumed they'd have years to work on it. Instead, Tut was placed in a small, cramped tomb already started for someone else. Into the tiny space were crammed bows, arrows, chariots, thrones, and anything else he would need in the afterlife. Seeds and herbs were added, as were food, bejeweled bowls, richly detailed plates, and golden goblets.

Meanwhile, the embalmers were busy preparing Tut's body for the long journey ahead of it. Egyptians believed the heart was a person's most important part and the center of his being, and it was never removed from a body. Other important organs, such as the liver and intestines, were placed in stone jars. The brain was thought to be just a waste of space and was simply removed. The body was wrapped in strips of white linen. Then resin (a thick, fragrant goo that oozes from trees such as pines and cedars) was poured over it.

A feast was held just outside the tomb as a last celebration before the underground chambers were sealed. The floral collars that the guests wore were placed behind the heavy stone doors before the doors were closed for the final time.

The History, Part 2: The Quick and Dirty Burial

Tut's early and unexpected death meant that an appropriate tomb was not yet ready for him. The walls of the tomb weren't beautifully decorated, as artists usually had time to do before a king died. Some of the rooms even seemed unfinished.

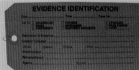
EVIDENCE IDENTIFICATION

Although Tut was young, he was a very rich king. This death mask, which was placed directly on his mummy, was made of gold, semiprecious stones, and colored glass stripes. There are many people who might have killed Tut for his wealth.

Many of the items in the treasury and annex rooms of the tomb likely belonged to someone else. It appeared obvious that other people's names had once been on some of the artifacts before those names were rubbed out and replaced with Tut's.

Some pieces of furniture in the tomb were broken, while others, including beds and shrines, were barely assembled. All the items looked like they'd been shoved into the tomb rather than placed there with care. Even the beautiful stone sarcophagus wasn't fit for a king. The lid didn't match the base, which showed how quickly it was assembled.

The forgotten tomb

Because Tut was such an insignificant king, his tomb was very small. That turned out to be a good thing. Tomb robbers broke into big, important tombs because the burglars knew the tombs would be full of priceless treasure. But they mostly ignored small tombs like Tut's. Although one or two robbers broke in to the young king's last resting place and took a few things, they were looking for more valuable loot. As years passed, the tomb was forgotten. The desert winds covered it with sand until the steps down to Tut's final resting place were completely buried. For thousands of years, the boy king waited in the silent darkness …

Carter's amazing discovery

In November 1922, archaeologist Howard Carter was running out of luck. He'd been searching for the tomb of a little-known king in Egypt's Valley of the Kings for seven years, but success had eluded him. Some experts believed there were no tombs left undiscovered there.

However, Carter had seen artifacts from the area that bore the mark of a minor king named Tutankhamun. The archaeologist was convinced this king was entombed in the Valley of the Kings, still waiting to be found. Now, with funding remaining for just one more season from his patron, Lord Carnarvon, Carter was still coming up empty-handed.

Then, on November 4, one of his water carriers discovered a set of stairs that other archaeologists had overlooked. They led down into the ground, far below the desert sands. Carter and his team excavated the 16 steps down to a sealed doorway at the bottom. Then they gasped. Not only was there a royal seal on the door showing a king was buried on the other side, but also Carter and his workers could tell that grave robbers had barely disturbed this tomb. Who knew what treasures might still be inside.

Carnarvon joined Carter, and the digging continued. Behind the sealed door lay a passage filled with stone and rubble. Clearing

THE MUMMY'S CURSE?

People were fascinated by the discoveries in Tut's tomb (shown above as it looks today), especially when rumors spread that his tomb was cursed. The stories started shortly after the tomb was found, when Lord Carnarvon, who had financed the expedition, became ill and died. But many others who helped discover the tomb or visited it lived long lives. The idea of a curse caught people's imagination, and it's still believed by some today.

the hallway revealed another sealed door, this one marked with the royal seal of Tutankhamun. Carter had found his missing king at last. But was the tomb as intact as it seemed?

On November 26, Carter and Carnarvon finally broke through a small hole in the second sealed door. The breach was just large enough for Carter to thrust a candle into the chamber on the other side and peer into the darkness. He was amazed at what lay before them. When Carnarvon asked him if he could see anything, all the astonished Carter could gasp was, "Yes, wonderful things!"

Carter was stunned by the statues of figures and animals he could see, especially the gold. It seemed to glisten and gleam from every artifact. But there was more to this tomb than just this one room. Beyond it was another, smaller room, also filled with treasures of gold, ivory, and intricately carved wood.

It took the team of archaeologists two and a half months to make a record of all the fantastic artifacts in the two rooms. Luckily, they took photographs as they worked, because items such as garlands of flowers disintegrated the moment they were touched. It was painstaking work, but finally, on February 16, 1923, Carter and his team were ready to break through another sealed door they'd discovered.

The burial chamber

At first, Carter thought this new room held a gold wall because that's all he could see. But when his workers removed more of the doorway, they realized they'd found the massive golden shrine that held the tomb's mummy.

The huge shrine was about as large as a medium-sized room. It would take years to catalog its vast contents. First were the four gilded wooden boxes that enclosed the granite sarcophagus or casket. Inside the sarcophagus were three coffins, one inside the other. The outer two were wooden, but the inmost one was gold. Pure gold.

On October 28, 1925, Carter and his team opened that phenomenal final coffin. Inside lay King Tutankhamun's mummy,

If the tomb is intact, what does it say about the king and his times?

EVIDENCE IDENTIFICATION

Tut's tomb was full of priceless treasure in a surprisingly messy jumble. Experts wondered if grave robbers had caused the chaos or if Tut had died—or been murdered—so unexpectedly that his tomb had to be hastily prepared.

resting beneath an unbelievable golden and bejeweled death mask. Carter couldn't believe his eyes. That priceless mask is now the most famous icon of ancient Egypt.

Today, the mummy beneath the fabulous mask and royal jewelry is as valuable to archaeologists as the gems and riches that surrounded him. But in Carter's time, that wasn't true. Carter knew that word would spread quickly about his incredible discovery. If he left the fantastic mask in the tomb for even one night, by morning it would likely be stolen. Somehow, he had to remove the mask from the mummy.

But Tut's body was covered with more resin than Howard Carter had ever seen on a mummy. The thick goo glued Tut's body to the coffin, and Carter and his staff couldn't figure out how to detach it.

First they carried the mummy out of the tomb into the hot

Egyptian sun to try to melt the rock-hard resin. That didn't work. All it did was "bake" the mummy. Then the workers chipped and hacked at the resin with hot knives. That didn't work much better.

Eventually, Carter and his team resorted to actually dismembering the body to chisel it out of the coffin. They cut off the arms and legs, severed the head, and sliced the torso in two. When they couldn't remove the large, priceless necklace from Tut's rib cage, they simply ripped the bones off with it.

Archaeologists today would be horrified, and the effect on the mummy was disastrous. It began to deteriorate rapidly, especially what was left of the soft tissue. Carter caused further damage when he moved the fragile bones and propped them up for photographs before laying them out again in the coffin.

More treasure

There were still two more rooms in Tut's tomb to explore and catalog. In the room now known as the treasury, workers found more than 5,000 artifacts, estimated to be worth more than $50 billion in today's dollars. In the room called the annex, archaeologists discovered about 2,000 items, mostly jars and bottles of food, wine, oils, and ointments.

One of the most curious finds was a huge collection of canes or walking sticks. There were around 130 of them, the largest collection ever found in a royal tomb. Carter and his workers couldn't imagine why a king as young as Tut could possibly want that many.

The walking sticks were yet another mystery surrounding this young king's life—and death …

The Clues: Scanning the Past

The sun glowered behind dark clouds in January 2005 as the team of investigators appeared out of the gloom of King Tutankhamun's tomb. Squinting in the daylight, they took time to allow their eyes to adjust. They mustn't drop the priceless burden they carried.

FACE THE FACTS

CT scans also help forensic scientists create an image of how a crime victim might have looked. If all that's left of a corpse is the skeleton, it can be hard to identify the person. But if police can build a model of the victim's face, then the public may be able to recognize the person.

A police artist starts with CT scans of living people, which show where bones cast shadows and how deep skin and tissue are at various points. An image of the victim's skull is brought up on the computer. Then it's merged with an image of a living person's skull to approximate the correct tissue depth. Any clothing found with the skull is examined to get a sense of whether the victim was thin or fat, and therefore how much tissue to add to the face.

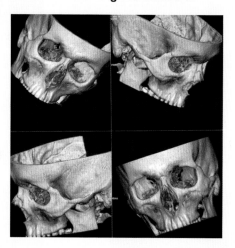

Of course, CT scans can't tell researchers the victim's skin, hair, or eye color, but they can help with estimating the victim's age. Many skeletons have been identified thanks to images created using CT scans.

Then, gingerly, they stepped forward, bearing the 3,000-year-old mummy up the 16 stone steps, out of the damp of the underground chambers into the arid Egyptian desert. With great care, the wooden box where the mummy rested was placed in a waiting van.

Inside the van was a mobile CT scanner, a state-of-the-art medical imaging tool that researchers hoped would help them unlock the mummy's many secrets. This was one of the few machines they could use on such a delicate artifact, since CT scanning is noninvasive and would cause the mummy no damage. The mummy had been X-rayed in the late 1960s and 1970s, but the CT scans would give researchers their first detailed, three-dimensional view of Tut, inside and out.

The workers painstakingly unwrapped the layers of linen surrounding the king. Over the years, the mummy had been badly damaged by age, atmosphere, and even archaeologists. No one wanted to cause it any further injuries.

Finally, the team removed the last strips of cloth and gazed at the blackened, leathery mummy. Very few people had ever seen the actual mummy. It was usually safely hidden deep in its covered stone sarcophagus. It was cautiously placed in the CT scanner, and a medical doctor moved into place to start the scanning.

As the team watched, the scanner began shooting the first of hundreds of images. The workers relaxed as everything proceeded according to schedule.

Then suddenly the machine stopped!

The workers stared at one another in confusion. What had happened? They all knew about the legendary curse of King Tut, but that was just a myth—wasn't it? Or was the ancient king now showing his displeasure at being disturbed? If the scanner was broken, would their months of preparation be useless? Or worse—would the curse strike them all dead?

After a long moment, the machine finally started to hum again. Everyone gave a sigh of relief and anxiously watched the scanner for signs of any more problems.

FACE FROM THE PAST

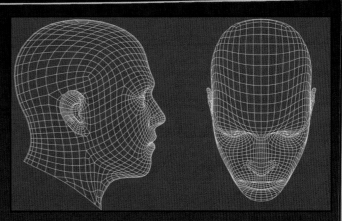

In 2005, three teams of forensic artists from Egypt, France, and the United States were given Tut's CT scans and asked to produce a 3-D model of his head. Both the Egyptian and French teams knew they were working with scans of the boy king, but the Americans were left in the dark.

Despite this, it was surprising how similar the 3-D faces looked. Each one appeared quite baby-faced, with chubby cheeks, a rounded forehead, and large eyes. Like the rest of his family, Tut had buck teeth, a pointy head, a weak chin, and a large nose.

CRIME-SOLVER

CT scans can help detectives solve many different kinds of crime, not just murders. The scans are used to identify stolen antiques and paintings or to confirm whether they are real or fake. These scans are a valuable tool for experts working with priceless artifacts because they allow a complete examination without damaging the items.

And King Tut wasn't the first mummy to be scanned. Other Egyptian mummies have been scanned, as well as a 5,200-year-old mummy found frozen in the Italian Alps. X-rays didn't show the fatal arrowhead in his body, but the CT scan did.

After just 15 minutes, it was all over. But for many of the team, the work had just begun. Now there were 1,700 cross-section images of the mummy for the researchers to study. The team hoped the CT scans would answer the many questions they had about King Tut, including the biggest one: How did he die?

How do CT scans help solve crimes?

CT scans have told researchers a lot about King Tut, but this high-tech medical tool was actually developed in the 1970s to help living patients. These scans can show tumors, look at organs and bones, or help doctors map out procedures for upcoming surgery.

During a CT scan, an X-ray device moves around the entire body, creating cross-section slides. These images are then fed into a computer to make 3-D images. CT stands for computed tomography; the Greek word *tomos* means "slice."

Like any X-ray imaging machine, a CT scanner shoots a beam of X-rays at the body. But CT scans can tell doctors much more than X-rays can. Bones and tissues (especially internal organs and blood vessels) can be seen much more clearly in a CT scan.

As the X-ray beams pass through the body, different tissues absorb various amounts of the radiation. Bones absorb lots of energy and look white. Skin, fat, and muscle absorb less energy and appear gray. Lungs are filled with air, which makes them take in almost no energy and appear black.

Forensic scientists use CT scanning to solve crimes, especially murder cases. CT scans show wounds and other injuries that can't be seen in a regular autopsy. Forensic scientists find this scanning most useful in deaths caused by bullets or blows to the body.

With a CT scan, detectives can examine skull and brain injuries and find bullets, bullet fragments, and bone fragments embedded in the brain. A CT scan can trace the path of the bullet, show how the brain was damaged, where bleeding occurred, and more.

About the only murders that CT scans can't help solve are poison cases. CT scans can also help identify victims of natural disasters

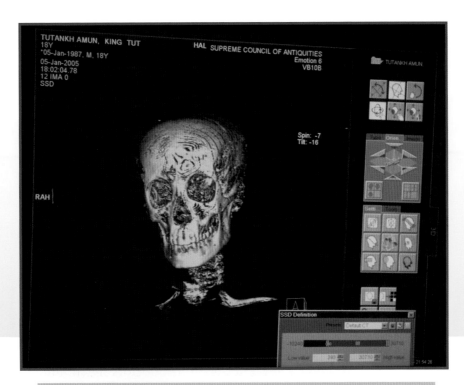

CT scans like this one of King Tut's head helped scientists move closer to solving a mystery that was more than 3,000 years old. The scans revealed clues that had been hidden since Tut's death.

or traffic accidents, and the scans also provide documentation in a form that can easily be stored or shared with others. Detectives often use CT scans in court when giving evidence. They can be a lot less gruesome than photos.

The scan unravels the mystery

The researchers were delighted by how much the CT scans of Tut's mummy told them about the ancient king. For one thing, the scans revealed that Tut suffered from Kohler disease, which affects a bone on the inside of the foot. The disease causes the bone to lose its blood supply, which kills tissue in the bone and makes it collapse. If Kohler disease is untreated, walking becomes agonizingly painful. The CT scans also showed that Tut had a clubfoot, which means it

was rotated inward at the ankle. It would have made him look as if he was walking on his ankle or on the side of his foot.

Neither the Kohler disease nor the clubfoot could have killed Tut, but they would have weakened him. They also explain the 130 walking sticks—Tut depended on them to get around.

The CT scans also told the Egyptologists a lot about Tut's mouth. He had buck teeth (which ran in his family) and an impacted wisdom tooth. Tut's wisdom teeth were in the process of coming in, something that usually happens when a person is between 18 and 20. This confirmed that the king died at about age 19. What researchers also didn't know before the scans was that Tut had a cleft palate, or a gap in the roof of his mouth. It likely gave him a slight lisp.

When the scientists examined the scans of Tut's broken left thigh bone, they saw no signs of bruising or healing. That likely meant that the break happened just before Tut died. It could have caused a severe infection. Combined with Tut's other health problems, it would have been enough to kill him. Perhaps Tut's weak, painful feet caused him to fall, or maybe he was hurt in a chariot accident.

It's also possible that the break was caused by Tut's embalmers when they were preparing his body. Experts believe that those workers were responsible for the bone fragments in his skull and that the chips weren't caused by a blow to his head. The scans showed that the chips weren't glued to the inside of the skull by the resin. They likely were broken off by Carter, or possibly by the embalmers centuries earlier.

DNA detectives

DNA typing (page 136), another modern medical technique like CT scanning, has also exposed some of Tut's secrets. DNA, or deoxyribonucleic acid, is the blueprint of genetic material that your cells receive from your parents and that makes you unique. At first, doctors weren't certain they would be able to extract usable DNA from such an ancient subject. However, thanks to

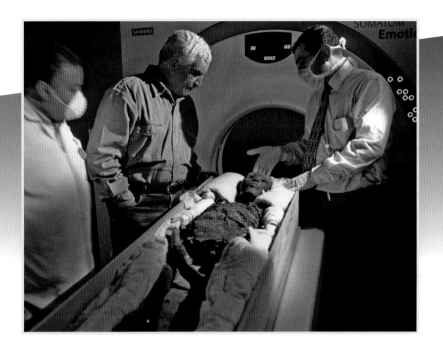

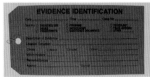
Here is part of the team that performed the CT scans on Tut's mummy in 2005. The scans gave researchers and archaeologists lots of new information, especially about Tut's leg and foot bones and his mouth.

embalming procedures used by Egyptian priests thousands of years earlier, researchers found DNA they could examine.

It's a lot tougher to analyze mummy DNA than a living person's DNA. The practice of embalming helped preserve the mummy DNA, but the process used breaks down its genetic material. It's also easy for any DNA to become contaminated over the thousands of years since the person died. One way of extracting "clean" DNA is to thoroughly clean one of the mummy's teeth, then drill to the inner pulp and extract the DNA there.

Perhaps the most important thing Tut's DNA proved was that his mother and father were also brother and sister. Marrying a sibling was common in Egyptian royal families, but because siblings are so genetically similar, it makes for unhealthy offspring. Tut is proof of that: he was probably weak and sickly most of his life.

X-ray evidence

Does a bone fragment in the skull always mean murder?

The first real evidence that Tut might have been assassinated had come in 1968 when the first X-rays of his mummy were created. They seemed to show a bone fragment in his skull. It could have been due to a fall, or an accident during mummification. But for many years, some people believed it was evidence of a fatal blow to his head. The X-ray also showed what looked like a blood clot at the skull's base—which for some time was thought to be evidence of a head injury.

The Suspects: Surrounded by Assassins?

There seemed to be evidence of murder, but who would have wanted Tut dead? Unfortunately for the boy king, lots of people. Most of them were very close to him and had plenty of opportunity to do him harm.

"Politically, we gather that the king's reign and life must have been a singularly uneasy one," said Howard Carter, who discovered Tut's tomb. "It may be that he was the tool of obscure political forces working behind the throne."

One likely suspect was Tut's prime minister, Ay. Everybody, including Tut, knew that Ay was much better at running the country than the king was. Perhaps Ay wondered why Tut was getting all the glory, while Ay was doing all the work. In fact, Ay did become king after Tut. If he had murdered the king to take the throne, his plot was successful. And as the government's most powerful official, it was easy for Ay to cover up his crime.

Tut's other main adviser, Horemheb, his military commander, is another potential murderer. While he could have used the soldiers under his command to battle for Egypt's crown, he may have preferred to get rid of Tut more quietly and secretly. Horemheb became king after Ay. Did he murder Tut to gain the power he craved?

Even Tut's wife, Ankhesenamen, might have wanted him dead.

EVIDENCE IDENTIFICATION

Was the person closest to Tut—his wife—also his murderer? In the image above, Ankhesenamen (on the right), is offering him flowers as a sign of love. But she would have had many opportunities to murder her husband.

She seemed to love him, but perhaps she wanted a new husband, one who could give her the child she desired. Ankhesenamen might also have had hopes of ruling in Tut's place.

All of these suspects saw Tut every day and had the opportunity to kill him. Nobody knows how Tut broke his leg, but even if a chariot accident caused the fatal fracture, the murderer might have sabotaged the chariot or deliberately scared the horses.

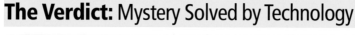

In 2010, Egyptologists made another amazing discovery. They discovered in Tut's mummy the DNA of the most life-threatening strain of malaria known. Malaria is a dangerous tropical disease that's passed along through mosquito bites. The symptoms are high fevers and headaches. In severe cases, a victim slips into a coma and then dies.

A diagnosis of malaria in Tut's case would explain a lot about his tomb and burial, such as the broken bones, excess resin, and lack of ceremony. He might have been buried quickly if the people around him thought malaria was contagious. Today, we know it's not, but ancient Egyptians may not have been aware of this.

Malaria might also have been the reason for some of the herbs and seeds found in Tut's tomb. The seeds were coriander, which ancient Egyptian doctors used to treat fever. The malaria, combined with the problem in his foot and perhaps an infection from a broken leg, could have been enough to kill the young man.

The mystery of Tutankhamun's death has been solved, thanks to modern science. We now know that Tut's bones left him weak and in intense pain, but that severe malaria killed him. His murderer wasn't a jealous official or unhappy wife after all, but a mosquito.

Though he wasn't important during his lifetime, Tut became the most famous king in Egyptian history when Carter found his tomb in 1922. Since Tut's tomb was relatively undisturbed, it gave archaeologists amazing insights into how ancient Egyptians lived.

The questions surrounding Tut's death have kept people fascinated by the young king and have given him exactly what he wanted: immortality. Egyptians from Tut's time believed that to speak a person's name is to make him live again. These ancient people didn't want to ever be forgotten. They wanted their names read and spoken forever. People are sure to be talking about King Tutankhamun far into the future.

MURDEROUS MOSQUITO

It's likely Tut wasn't the first royal to die from malaria. This disease has killed kings and commoners for more than 50,000 years. About half of the world's population is still at risk of catching malaria, especially people living in Africa below the Sahara Desert.

Malaria was once also common in the United States and southern Europe, including Italy. In fact, the name *malaria* ("bad air") comes from ancient Italian and was given to this disease thanks to the smelly air of the swamps where malaria mosquitoes live.

Malaria is caused by a parasite that's passed along in the bite of a particular type of mosquito. These dangerous fliers are active at night, so sleeping under an insecticide-treated net is a good way to help avoid malaria.

Nearly one million people die from malaria each year, but numerous groups are working to stop the disease. Malaria mosquitoes have been eliminated from many parts of the world, including North America (Canada and the United States) and most of Europe.

LOST PRINCE

What Was the Fate of Marie-Antoinette's Son?

CRIME SCENE

June 8, 1795, Temple prison, Paris, France

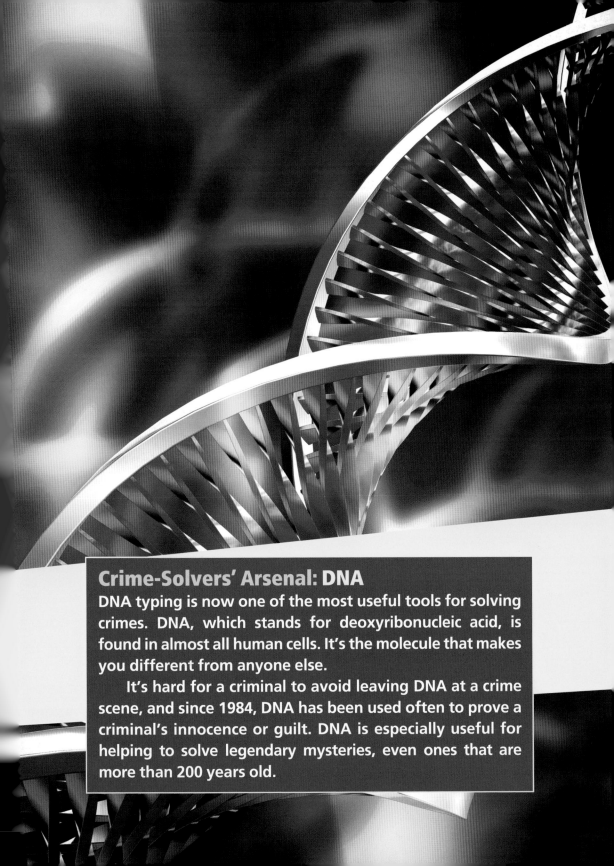

Crime-Solvers' Arsenal: DNA

DNA typing is now one of the most useful tools for solving crimes. DNA, which stands for deoxyribonucleic acid, is found in almost all human cells. It's the molecule that makes you different from anyone else.

It's hard for a criminal to avoid leaving DNA at a crime scene, and since 1984, DNA has been used often to prove a criminal's innocence or guilt. DNA is especially useful for helping to solve legendary mysteries, even ones that are more than 200 years old.

The Mystery: A Royal Funeral?

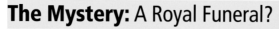

A hush fell over Saint-Denis Basilica, in northern Paris. It was June 8, 2004, and thousands of royals, nobles, and aristocrats somberly gathered in the huge church. Many wore black, with gold crosses and other elaborate jewelry. These aristocrats had traveled from all over Europe to finally lay to rest France's boy king, Louis XVII, who was believed to have died exactly 209 years earlier when he was just 10 years old.

A crowd of royal supporters watched the ceremony on a huge screen outside. Earlier, their cameras had clicked and flashed as a hearse pulled up to the huge cathedral. The black vehicle was brimming with white lilies, the flower symbolic of French royalty, and their scent still hung thick in the air.

A crystal vase was carefully removed from the hearse and taken into the basilica. Then a slim young boy slowly and reverently walked up the cathedral's main aisle. He was Prince Amaury de Bourbon-Parme, descendant of France's former royal family, and he carried the crystal vase draped with a royal purple cloth. The rich fabric was heavily embroidered with golden fleurs-de-lis, another symbol of French royals. In the vase was a tiny, rock-hard object. It was hard to believe it had once been a little boy's heart. But this was all that remained of Louis XVII.

With trumpets blaring, bells ringing, and incense swirling, the vase containing the heart was carefully placed next to a crown in France's royal crypt, close to the graves of his parents, King Louis XVI and Queen Marie-Antoinette. The heart had been positively identified as belonging to Louis XVII. The 200-year-old mystery surrounding his death and what had happened to his body was finally solved.

Or was it?

That heart had had a long, strange journey to this basilica. The twists and turns included theft, a riot, trips across Europe, and more. After all these years, could this actually be the heart of

This is how the heart believed to be Louis XVII's looked in its crystal case when it was placed in the royal crypt. The heart was treated as if it belonged to one of France's royals—but did it?

Louis XVII? And was it really Marie-Antoinette's son who had died all those years ago?

The History, Part 1: Imprisoned!

King Louis XVI and Queen Marie-Antoinette of France were delighted with their youngest son. Born March 27, 1785, Louis-Charles was a healthy, clever, carefree little boy. His long blond curls and big blue eyes made him everyone's favorite. No wonder he was happy—he was a prince, but because he had an older brother, he would never have to be king and cope with the responsibility of governing his country.

However, when Louis-Charles was just four years old, his brother, Louis-Joseph, died. That meant suddenly Louis-Charles was next in line to the French throne.

But about a month later, the French Revolution broke out. This was a battle that pitted France's aristocracy against the common people and intellectuals. In 1792, the French royal family, including King Louis, Queen Marie-Antoinette, Louis-Charles, and his sister Marie Thérèse, were imprisoned in the ancient Temple prison. The great tower of the prison loomed over the streets of Paris below, and the thick walls ensured no prisoner would ever escape.

Louis, as his family called him, and his father, the king, were imprisoned on the second floor, while his mother and sister were on the floor above. They all lived behind double doors that were locked and guarded night and day. The servants who cleaned the rooms and brought the royal family their food were actually revolutionaries and spies, who were eager to report anything the royals did or said.

In December 1792, Louis was moved to his mother's chamber. Then, on January 20, 1793, he saw his father for the last time. The next day, the king was beheaded and Louis became, at least according to the group supporting the royals, King Louis XVII.

On the night of July 3, 1793, six guards burst into the queen's room. They demanded that the queen turn her little son over to them. She refused and clung to her only boy. It wasn't until the guards threatened to kill both Louis and his sister that the soldiers were finally able to tear Louis away from his mother.

The terrified boy was moved back to his old room on the second floor where he'd stayed with his father. But now only Louis was left. His tutor was a shoemaker named Antoine Simon, but all Simon taught Louis were bad manners, songs about the Revolution, and how to swear. Simon's job was to make Louis lose all idea of being special and royal.

Simon bullied the boy and made the now-king wait on him like a servant. The shoemaker beat Louis, sometimes just because he felt like it. Despite the bad treatment, some people claimed that

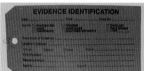

EVIDENCE IDENTIFICATION

France's Queen Marie-Antoinette was terrified when her son, Louis-Charles, was taken from her in July 1793. What would happen to him? His fate would be a mystery for more than 200 years.

Louis was still well fed, clothed, and clean. After all, the aim of the revolutionaries was to figure out the best way to use him in their campaign, not to kill or harm him.

Beginning of the end

Although Louis's mother was guillotined on October 16, 1793, Louis was never told. Soon, more things began to change for him. In early January 1794, Simon was fired and forced to leave the tower immediately.

Until then, lots of people had seen Louis: friends of Simon's, revolutionaries, guards, and almost anyone else who wanted to have a look at the imprisoned king. But now, the boy was completely

What might the fact that the revolutionaries sometimes treated Louis well and sometimes badly say about how and when he died?

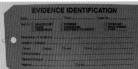
Sometimes Louis XVII was well cared for by his jailer, Simon, and other times the boy was bullied and beaten by the man. After Simon was fired, life became even worse for little Louis.

isolated. He was moved into a windowless dungeon with a hatch in the door. The guards could shove food into the cell without having to open the door.

With no visitors or companions, the little prisoner spent most of his days lying in his bed, which quickly became filthy and crawling with bugs. He learned to leave some leftovers from his meals so the rats would fight over them and leave him alone.

This is where the reports about the youngster begin to conflict with one another, and the mystery surrounding his end begins. Some guards said Louis was clean and well dressed. Others said he barely had the strength to stand and his dungeon stank. Another official said he tried to get the child to speak, but he wouldn't say a word.

The History, Part 2: Death of the Boy Prisoner

By May 1795, it was obvious to Louis's jailers that their small prisoner was dying. All the boy's doctor, Pierre-Joseph Desault, could do was gently try to relieve his suffering. The little boy grabbed the doctor's coat sleeve and begged, "Please do not leave me among these wicked men!"

But this kindly doctor died shortly (and mysteriously; see page 136) after his last visit to the prison. In the first week of June, Dr. Philippe-Jean Pelletan became the boy's doctor. Pelletan was a revolutionary—and a spy. He often tried to find out any political secrets about his patients as he treated them. This second doctor quickly realized Louis was fatally ill and simply recommended nourishing food and better conditions in the dungeon.

No one was surprised when the little boy died on June 8, 1795. But the jailors tried to keep his death secret. A guard who might have let the truth slip was shut up in one of the prison's cells. While one guard left to ask for instructions from the revolutionaries, the other ordered medicine and broth to be delivered as if Louis were still alive.

The History, Part 3: Missing Pieces and Persons

When Pelletan asked to see the dead body, he was told he'd be allowed to but that he would then also have to remain in the prison. Then, the revolutionaries decided Pelletan and two more doctors would dissect the child the next day to try to discover what killed him. Meanwhile, the jailors kept acting as if Louis were still alive.

The greedy doctor

When the doctors began their autopsy, the stench in the room was terrible. The body had already begun to putrefy. Pelletan was used to performing dissections and autopsies, so the other doctors quickly decided to let him do most of the work. Meanwhile, they stood by the open window, trying to get a breath of fresh air.

What can the type of grave say about a person's life?

Pelletan kept an eye on the other doctors, waiting for a moment when neither of them was watching him. Then, in a flash, he stole the child's heart! The doctor quickly wrapped it in a handkerchief and slipped it into his pocket. Finally, he sewed up the body of the little king who never ruled. The doctors agreed the poor small boy had died of what today would be called tuberculosis, a lung disease.

But the autopsy left the body almost beyond identification. Illness had made Louis deformed and emaciated. After the dissection, a large bandage had to be wrapped around his head to hold the skin and skull together. Although a number of officers and guards signed a statement late that evening that this was indeed Louis's corpse, it's unlikely they really recognized him. Was it really Louis?

A not-so-royal burial

The guards later reported that the next evening the little body was placed in a coffin. It was buried in a hole that wasn't much more than an open trench, just a common grave for the poor. One soldier stood guard at the grave and another at the cemetery gate to prevent the grave from being disturbed.

At least, that's what one story claimed about the burial. Rumors flew. Another story made the rounds that on June 13, 1795, revolutionaries had buried the body in a different graveyard altogether. A gravedigger claimed that both these stories were wrong and that he'd dug up the coffin and reburied it in a more proper grave. Others said the coffin had been buried only once, and not in a common pit but in a special unmarked grave.

It was just a few days after the little prisoner's death and already there was mystery about it. Was it possible that a king of France could really be buried in such a humble grave? What if it wasn't even Louis who had been buried?

The heart of the story

After the autopsy of the poor wasted little body, Dr. Pelletan hurried home. There, he placed the heart he'd stolen in a crystal vase that

Artists later drew Louis-Charles in his prison cell but they didn't really know how he looked at this point. That's because so few people saw him after January 1794.

he'd filled with alcohol to help preserve his grisly memento. This might seem strange now, but at the time, there was a tradition of preserving royal hearts separate from their bodies. To make sure no one else saw the heart, he hid it behind books on the topmost shelf of his library.

But Pelletan was a very busy doctor. He soon forgot all about the heart.

Eight or ten years later, Pelletan suddenly remembered his royal relic. But when he pulled out the vase, he was horrified to find that the alcohol was long gone and the heart had completely dried out. The doctor removed it from the vase and dumped it in his desk. He was scared that revolutionaries might think he was a royalist if they knew he had the heart of the young king, so he told no one—except one of his students, Dr. Tillus.

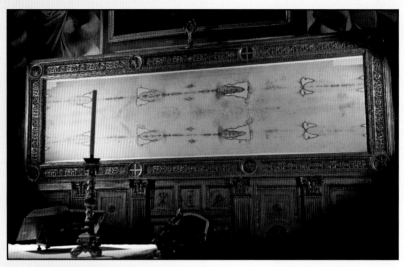

Some think this relic is a shroud that once covered Jesus Christ.

HOLY HEART!

It isn't just people in France who stored away special body parts or relics. People from many cultures and religions have collected them for thousands of years. The word *relic* comes from a Latin word meaning "remains."

A relic can range from something a royal, saint, or holy person may have touched (like a book or clothing) to a body part (including hair, a bone, or an arm) to a whole body. Some people think praying to religious relics makes their prayers more powerful and can even result in miracles.

That was a mistake. Because when Pelletan again looked for the heart a few years later, it was missing. Since only one person knew he had it, then that was the person who must have stolen it. Tillus no longer worked for Pelletan. The old doctor finally tracked him down, but it was too late. Tillus had just died.

But the theft of the heart had haunted the student to his deathbed. As he lay dying, Tillus confessed and begged his wife to return the heart to Pelletan. She gave Pelletan a little purse containing the heart. But was it the real one? After all these years? Pelletan had no doubts. He said he immediately recognized "the object he had seen and touched more than a thousand times."

Pelletan held on to the heart until 1814, when the royal family was back in power in France. He tried to return the heart to Louis XVIII, the king who now sat on the country's throne. But the new king wasn't sure that the heart had really belonged to Louis XVII and doubted Pelletan's intentions. He refused to accept it.

When Charles X took over the throne in 1824, Pelletan tried again. But this time, he got the archbishop of Paris involved. The archbishop agreed to keep the heart, now back in a crystal container, in his library until he could convince the king to take it.

Then disaster! In July 1830, there was a riot in Paris and the archbishop's residence was trashed. One rioter saw the crystal vase and grabbed it, not knowing or caring what was inside. Another rioter saw the valuable-looking vase and tried to wrestle it from the first man. The second looter smashed the vase with his sword, which made the first one run from the room, taking only the sheaf of papers that had been with the vase.

When the rioter read those papers and discovered what was in the crystal vase, he returned to the archbishop's home to see if the heart was still there. He took time first to find Dr. Pelletan's son—the doctor had died years before—and the two of them eventually located the hard, dried little heart and plucked it out of the shards of glass all around it.

Pelletan's son and his descendants tried to convince Louis's

relatives to take the heart, but still none of them was convinced that it was authentic. Finally, in 1895, the family accepted the heart, and it traveled with family members to Venice, then to Austria and Italy, and finally back to France in 1975, when it was placed in the royal crypt in Saint-Denis Basilica.

However, this didn't mean that the heart had definitely belonged to Louis. The rocklike small piece of flesh was recognized only as the heart of the child who died in the Temple prison, but not necessarily that it had once belonged to the royal child.

The dauphin reappears

Because of the questions and puzzles surrounding Louis's death, it wasn't long after the sad event that boys claiming to be the prince, or dauphin, began to spring up.

One of the most famous started off rather badly by claiming he was Charles Louis, the lost king of France. Of course, the correct name was Louis-Charles! Despite this mistake, he soon had many supporters, even though he claimed to have forgotten French, which was the only language Louis had ever spoken, and had spent time in prison for forging money.

This claimant, who also went by the name Karl Wilhelm Naundorff, was recognized as Louis by some former servants of the royal family and by high-ranking officials. He seemed to know a lot about the palace of Versailles, where Louis lived before being imprisoned, and Naundorff did look a lot like Louis's family.

Naundorff described how he'd been rescued from Temple prison in November 1794 and hidden in the attics of the tower. A child who wasn't able to speak (and couldn't tell anyone who he really was) had been substituted in his place. That explained why an official had been unable to get the imprisoned child to say a word.

Then, just days before Louis supposedly died, that child was replaced with a dying child, who passed away only a few days later. Naundorff said he was smuggled out of the prison in the coffin that everyone assumed held the dead boy's body.

Louis and his family lived in the Palace of Versailles before the French Revolution. The palace includes the world-famous Hall of Mirrors. When it was built, mirrors were some of the most expensive items anyone could own.

On top of Naundorff's claim, other stories emerged about how Louis was spirited out of the prison. One guard stated he'd once seen many bathtubs being carried out of the prison. When a guard carrying one stumbled, the first guard claimed he heard a child's cry come from inside one of the tubs.

Louis's sister, Marie Thérèse, had survived the dreadful prison (the only one in her family who had) and denounced Naundorff as an imposter. She refused to have anything to do with him or his supporters. Naundorff then claimed that his real sister had been kidnapped, and this woman was an imposter!

When Naundorff died in Holland in 1845, his death certificate read "King Louis XVII of France" and his gravestone is engraved (in French) with the words *Louis XVII, King of France.* As recently as 60 years ago, his descendants were still going to court, trying to

receive recognition as France's royal family. Even today, supporters still claim that he was the real thing.

Dangerous doctoring

Remember the kindly doctor who treated the poor imprisoned boy just weeks before he died? That doctor, Pierre-Joseph Desault, didn't get a chance to write a lot of reports about his royal patient. Desault died shortly after his last visit to the royal child.

But, there is a story that claims Desault said the boy he'd treated in the Temple prison wasn't the dauphin. He believed that some other child had been substituted for Louis, but Desault was afraid of what the revolutionaries might do if they discovered he knew about the substitution. He shared his doubts only with his wife. But did the anti-royalists somehow find out anyway?

Some of Desault's relatives were convinced the revolutionaries decided to take no chances and poisoned the doctor. On the other hand, a deadly epidemic had swept through the hospital where Desault worked, and maybe he was just one of a number of doctors who died. Was Desault murdered, or was his death simply coincidental? And what did his death have to do with the puzzle surrounding Louis's death?

The Clues, Part 1: The Body's Blueprint

For many years, few clues were uncovered to help solve the mystery of Louis. Then medical technology offered some possibilities.

Back in 1869, scientists discovered the material that allows animals and plants to pass on characteristics to their offspring. DNA is like a blueprint or recipe: it contains the instructions needed for the development and functioning of living organisms. The human body contains a lot of DNA. Believe it or not, there is a stretch of DNA almost 1 meter (3 feet) long in every cell of your body! The DNA in all the cells in your body would stretch from Earth to Pluto and back.

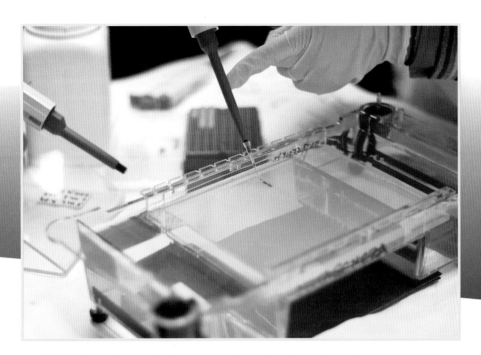

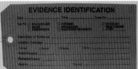
Once police or researchers obtain a DNA sample, it is processed in a lab so it can reveal its unique "fingerprint." If the sample can provide a clear and obvious fingerprint, then it's likely the DNA can be identified.

It wasn't until 1984 that scientists first began using DNA analysis to solve crimes, and it caused a revolution in forensic science. Experts discovered that most of a person's DNA is identical to every other person's. But the small amount that's different can be used to distinguish one person from another. Even identical twins have slightly different DNA. A DNA fingerprint is the same for every cell, tissue, and organ of a person. And there's no way that fingerprints can be changed.

Blood, bones, and hair

If detectives are dealing with crime suspects, they usually request a DNA sample from the potential criminal. A quick scrape of the inside of the cheek provides forensic scientists with the cells they need, and it's easy and painless for the suspect.

TYPES OF DNA

There are two types of DNA that forensic scientists can use to create a DNA fingerprint. One kind is called nuclear DNA. It's found in the nucleus of the cell, which is the part of the cell that controls its growth, reproduction, and more. Nuclear DNA is found in blood, semen, saliva, body tissues, and hair follicles.

Another part of the cell is called the mitochondrion, and it generates the cell's energy. Mitochondria contain their own DNA, which can also be used for profiling. It's found in hair, bones, and teeth. Forensic scientists often use mitochondrial DNA for identifying victims and suspects because there is usually lots of this type of DNA. That's because each cell contains many mitochondria and therefore many copies of mitochondrial DNA. But every cell has only one nucleus, so it has only one copy of nuclear DNA. Mitochondrial DNA also survives well over long periods of time.

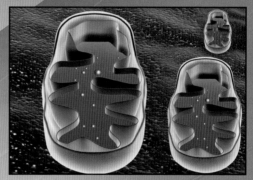

Cross section of Mitochondria

Mitochondrial DNA is unique because it is always inherited in the line of female relatives. This type of DNA has two particular areas that are very different if the two people don't share a female relative, and it's easy to prove whether the two people are likely related.

A new, super-sensitive DNA technology called low copy number (LCN) DNA allows scientists to create a DNA profile from an extremely small sample.

It can be fairly easy to obtain DNA for testing from the scene of a crime. You probably don't realize it, but you and everyone around you are constantly shedding DNA. There are about 3 trillion cells in the human body, but only about 100 are needed to obtain a DNA profile.

To identify a person, forensic scientists scan 13 DNA areas (scientists call them foci) that vary between people. The experts use the data they receive to create a DNA profile, or fingerprint, of that person. The chance that two people share the same DNA fingerprint for a particular set of 13 areas is almost zero.

Identifying the unidentifiable

At the scene of a crime, experts use DNA typing to identify the victim and anybody else who was there. DNA profiling can prove people are innocent of a suspected crime, establish a relationship between people, and prove who owned and/or touched or used items such as clothing, cars, weapons, and more. In all of these cases, the DNA has to be protected from such things as weather, animals, and traffic in order to be typed and used for identification.

Not only can DNA analysis solve many modern crimes, but it can also help solve ancient ones. For instance, DNA testing is providing information about King Tut's family and his mysterious death (page 116). It also solved the puzzle of Russia's Romanov family and whether they were all murdered (page 78). Forensic experts will soon even be able to reconstruct facial features and skin just by reading DNA. We may learn how long-dead famous people looked, even if their faces have been mysteries for centuries.

The Clues, Part 2: The Clue in the Heart

In 1999, scientists decided to use DNA technology to try to solve the mystery of the identity of the heart. First, the heart was studied by an expert in anatomy, which is the study of the body's structure. This scientist said the heart had belonged to a child who'd died

TOUCH DNA

At a crime scene, scientists check for DNA in samples from blood, bone, hair, and other body tissues found nearby. Experts can also analyze saliva on cigarettes, rims of cups and glasses, and even stamps, to create a DNA profile. Criminals can be identified merely from traces of "touch DNA" left in fingerprints at a crime scene.

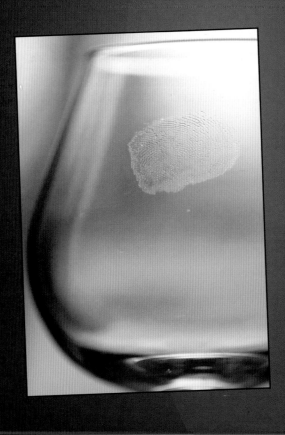

somewhere between the ages of 5 and 12 years old. Louis had been 10 when he passed away.

At first, scientists wondered if they'd be able to analyze the heart's DNA since the heart was as hard as rock. As well, it had been stored in alcohol for many years, which might have destroyed vital tissue. To create samples for analysis, the heart had to be cut with a very sharp knife, but scientists were eventually able to remove some material for DNA testing and even create a DNA profile from the heart.

But to show that the heart belonged to a member of the French royal family, scientists would have to find samples from family members to compare the DNA. Luckily, hair samples of Louis's mother, Marie-Antoinette, had been kept from her childhood. Researchers also extracted DNA samples from her sisters, their mother, and two living relatives, a great-aunt and great-uncle of the young boy who carried the heart up the cathedral aisle to its final resting place.

Because these samples came from Louis's mother and her family, researchers could analyze the mitochondrial DNA in them. Although some of the samples were more than 200 years old, this type of DNA had survived well, and there was lots to examine.

When scientists compared the DNA from the heart with the DNA from Marie-Antoinette's hair, they found a match. The DNA from the heart showed the same variations as the DNA from Marie-Antoinette and all of her relatives. That proved beyond a shadow of a doubt that the heart belonged to a member of the French royal family.

What about Naundorff's DNA?

Remember that pretender, Karl Wilhelm Naundorff? When DNA taken from bone and hair found in his grave was compared with Marie-Antoinette's, no match was found. But that hasn't stopped Naundorff's descendants from continuing to push their claim for royal status.

Some of these would-be royals say the heart was contaminated over the years, so DNA testing is meaningless. Others claim it was switched with another heart during the 1900s, when it was traveling from family to family while different royals were looking after it. They also state that the samples from Naundorff's grave were contaminated before testing, and they asked for more testing.

The Clues, Part 3: Silence in the Tower

Even though DNA revealed that the heart Pelletan stole was likely royal, many historians still believe Louis was somehow rescued from the Temple prison and hidden. They say it happened around January 1794, and their proof is the change in his living conditions.

When his mother and sister last saw him in October 1793, they obviously would have realized immediately if another child had already replaced him. Then when Simon was Louis's jailer, Louis was seen by many people who would have noticed if another boy had been substituted for the prince. If he had been replaced, many people would have had to know about the change. It's not likely that everyone involved would have kept silent about it. And a daring rescue was unlikely because of all the guards in the tower.

But, there's no obvious reason why Louis was practically walled into his dungeon in January 1794. Unless, as some people have suggested, he'd been replaced and this had to be kept a secret.

An additional clue researchers pondered came from Marie Thérèse, Louis's sister. She claimed that on January 19, 1794, she'd heard a loud noise from the rooms on the floor below her, the ones where Louis was imprisoned. Was it Louis making a commotion about being moved? The young girl thought it was the sound of Louis getting transferred out of his cell and another prisoner being forced into it.

It's possible that Marie Thérèse got mixed up and was wrong about what she heard. But after months of being locked in the tower, with little to do but listen, Marie Thérèse was probably very good at

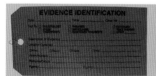
Marie-Antoinette (above, left) died in 1793. She never knew what happened to her son, Louis-Charles (right). Yet her DNA held clues to identifying the heart that for years many believed had belonged to him.

identifying the sounds of the prison. She also said that after the day she heard all the noise, she could no longer hear her brother yelling.

The tower became silent as death, and Marie Thérèse was convinced her brother had been taken away. Perhaps she was right. It seems strange, but for the first few months of 1794, there are no records in the prison about Louis. If he was still there, why were there no reports on his food, activities, and other items? If a commoner had been substituted for him, no one would be bothered to keep records about the substitute.

Why do people think a boy may have been substituted for Louis? One reason, perhaps, is that they want to believe it. It would mean that he escaped the prison and didn't die a sad, painful death. Other historians suggest that the royalists somehow rescued the little boy, but the revolutionaries didn't want to admit they'd lost him. They substituted another child to keep the escape a secret. Louis was a valuable pawn to both the royalists and the revolutionaries, and he was much more valuable alive than dead.

Once the rumors of a substitution started, they spread quickly. Eventually it was hard to know where the stories ended and the truth began.

Everything comes out in the wash

Historians looked at every piece of evidence they could find to try to solve the mystery of when Louis died. For instance, one researcher had a theory that the royal boy died in early January 1794. The proof? When the expert scoured the laundry records, he found the number of socks washed and delivered to the prison was lower than in previous weeks. Obviously, the historian said, there were fewer socks because there was one less child wearing them.

However, other researchers pored over the same records and found the number of shirts didn't change, so this theory had to be discarded. Besides, by this point, Louis was too ill to walk or even stand, and likely didn't need as many socks as he had before.

The Verdict: Definitely DNA

DNA testing proved that the heart resting in Saint-Denis Basilica belonged to a child related to Marie-Antoinette, but not necessarily to one of her children. Marie-Antoinette had 10 sisters who all would have had similar DNA, as would all of those sisters' children.

Most of these women not only married but also married royalty. Many of these royals, when they died, would have had their hearts preserved, since that was the custom of the time. It's possible that

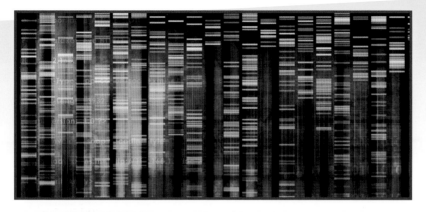

Here are the DNA fingerprints of a number of people. Researchers can distinguish and interpret the differences between these fingerprints to identify victims, criminals—and sometimes even long-dead royals.

any of these hearts could have been substituted for the little heart from the Temple prison, either deliberately or accidentally. From 1895 to 1975, the heart was in the safekeeping of royal relatives, which could have allowed lots of opportunity for a substitution.

But these hearts would have been cared for properly and not allowed to dry to rocklike hardness, like the heart that was tested. Experts agree that the heart now in the royal crypt at the Saint-Denis Basilica once belonged to young Louis.

Even though this mystery is officially solved, many people still aren't satisfied. "I would have liked to believe the story that the child survived," said Prince Charles-Emmanuel de Bourbon-Parme, father of the young boy who carried Louis's heart up the aisle of Saint-Denis Basilica in 2004.

At least the DNA results finally made the descendants of Karl Wilhelm Naundorff give up their claims to France's throne, right? Wrong. "This is an enormous masquerade," said one of Naundorff's heirs, "a plot against my person and the history of France."

Glossary

archaeology: study of human society by finding and examining materials the society left behind, including artifacts; see also *forensic archaeology*

arsenic: poisonous substance, often used in insecticides and weed killers

artifacts: human-made objects, or the remains of them, that are characteristic of an earlier time or culture

assassination: sudden or secret murder, especially of someone of political importance

autopsy: inspection and dissection of a dead body to try to find out how the person died

ballistics: science or study of the motion of bullets, bombs, and so on

bayonet: knife or dagger attached to the muzzle of a rifle

cartridges: brass casings around bullets; each one contains a bullet as well as the powder that propels the bullet out of the gun

Colt .45: handgun that is small, yet powerful and heavy

contamination: in forensics, the addition of extra materials to evidence that can make it unusable

convict: person serving time in prison

crime scene: place where a crime has taken place

crypt: chamber, usually in a church, that is used as a burial place

CT scan: imaging method that uses X-ray images to create a three-dimensional picture of the inside of an object; *CT* stands for computed tomography; also known as CAT scan

dactyloscopy: study of fingerprints to try to identify who left them

deductive reasoning: working with evidence and facts to form conclusions

dental records: information about a person's teeth, including X-rays and other images, charts, information on fillings, and dentist's notes

deoxyribonucleic acid (DNA): molecule in a cell that contains instructions needed for the development and functioning of living organisms; everyone's DNA, even twins', is slightly different

detective: police officer or private investigator who obtains information and evidence to try to solve crimes

evidence: object, mark, or information that tells investigators something about a crime

fingerprinting: taking impressions of the lines on the tips of a person's fingers

forensic anthropologist: scientist who studies skeletons and bones to obtain information about how the victims died or how a crime was committed

forensic archaeology: branch of forensic science that uses skills normally used in archaeology to discover ancient evidence

forensic science: use of different sciences to solve crimes; also known as forensics

genes: chemicals that control the shape and growth of every living thing; the basic unit of heredity found in DNA

graphology: study of handwriting to identify who wrote it or to learn about the writer's personality

gunshot residue (GSR): tiny particles that are left on a shooter's hand by a bullet, cartridge, or gun

laser: device that produces a very intense beam of light; *laser* stands for "light amplification by stimulated emission of radiation"

massacre: slaughter or killing of a large number of people

mummy: dead human or animal body that has been specially preserved or embalmed; the ancient Egyptian process of mummification involved removing body organs and wrapping the body in fabric

odontology: science and study of teeth and the tissue around them

pathologist: medical doctor who studies the origin and causes of diseases and injuries

perpetrator: someone who commits a crime

poison: substance that kills people or makes them ill

questioned document examination (QDE): area of forensic science that involves examining documents, especially to help solve court cases

rigor mortis: stiffening of the body after death

royalist: person who supports royalty

sabotage: deliberate hidden damage to an object, or secret interference with a process to cause upset or destruction

sarcophagus: coffin usually cut from stone and often covered with carvings or other decorations

sixth sense: feeling or hunch that can't be confirmed by evidence

trace evidence: evidence that's transferred when different objects contact one another

X-ray: radiation that can penetrate solids, including bones

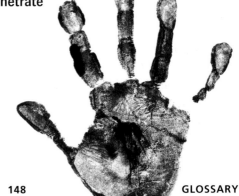

GLOSSARY

Main Sources

Forensics: The Key to History's Mysteries
Dulcie M. Ashdown. *Royal Murders: Hatred, Revenge and the Seizing of Power.* Stroud: Sutton Publishing, 1998.
Robert E. Bartholomew. *Hoaxes, Myths, and Manias.* Amherst: Prometheus Books, 2002.

Maya Royal Family
Michael D. Coe. *The Maya.* New York: Thames and Hudson, 2011.
Eva Eggebrecht. *Maya: Divine Kings of the Rain Forest.* Königswinter, Germany: H. F. Ullmann, 2007.
Timothy Laughton. *The Maya: Life, Myth, and Art.* London: Duncan Baird, 1998.
Robert J. Sharer. *Daily Life in Maya Civilization.* Westport, CT: Greenwood Press, 2009.
Peter A. Young. *Secrets of the Maya.* New York: Hatherleigh Press, 2003.

Napoleon Bonaparte
Bill Fawcett. *100 Mistakes that Changed History.* New York: Berkley Books, 2010.
Peter Haugen. *Was Napoleon Poisoned?* Hoboken: John Wiley & Sons, 2008.
Richard Platt. *Crime Scene.* New York: DK Publishing, 2003.
Robert Stewart. *Mysteries of History.* Washington: National Geographic Society, 2003.

The Man in the Iron Mask
Alexandre Dumas. *The Man in the Iron Mask.* New York: Penguin Books, 2003.
John Noone. *The Man Behind the Iron Mask.* New York: St. Martin's Press, 1988.
Harry Thompson. *The Man in the Iron Mask.* London: Weidenfeld & Nicolson, 1987.

King Rama VIII
Anthony Grey. *The Bangkok Secret.* London: Macmillan, 1990.
Rayne Kruger. *The Devil's Discus.* London: Cassell, 1964.
Richard Platt. *Forensics.* Boston: Kingfisher, 2005.
Keith Simpson. *Forty Years of Murder: An Autobiography.* London: Harrap, 1978.
William Stevenson. *The Revolutionary King.* London: Constable, 1999.

Grand Duchess Anastasia

Greg King and Penny Wilson. *The Fate of the Romanovs.* Hoboken, NJ: John Wiley & Sons, 2003.

Greg King and Penny Wilson. *The Resurrection of the Romanovs.* Hoboken, NJ: John Wiley & Sons, 2011.

Peter Kurth. *Anastasia: The Riddle of Anna Anderson.* Boston: Little, Brown, 1983.

James Blair Lovell. *Anastasia: The Lost Princess.* Washington: Regnery Gateway, 1994.

Robert K. Massie. *Nicholas and Alexandra.* New York: Atheneum, 1985.

Robert K. Massie. *The Romanovs: The Final Chapter.* New York: Random House, 1995.

Frances Welch. *A Romanov Fantasy: Life at the Court of Anna Anderson.* New York: W. W. Norton, 2007.

King Tutankhamun

Howard Carter. *The Tomb of Tutankhamen.* Washington: National Geographic Society, 2003.

Christine El Mahdy. *Tutankhamen.* New York: St. Martin's Griffin, 2001.

Michael King and Gregory Cooper. *Who Killed King Tut?* Amherst: Prometheus Books, 2004.

Louis XVII

Annunziata Asquith. *Marie Antoinette.* London: Weidenfeld & Nicolson, 1974.

Deborah Cadbury. *The Lost King of France.* London: St. Martin's Griffin, 2003

Michael Farquhar. *A Treasury of Royal Scandals.* New York: Penguin Books, 2001.

Antonia Fraser. *Marie Antoinette.* Toronto: Doubleday, 2001.

Joan Haslip. *Marie Antoinette.* London: Weidenfeld & Nicolson, 1989.

Stanley Burke-Roche Poole. *Royal Mysteries and Pretenders.* London: Blandford Press, 1969.

Munro Price. *The Road from Versailles.* New York: St. Martin's Press, 2003.

Further Reading

Forensics: The Key to History's Mysteries
Jan Bondeson. *The Great Pretenders.* New York: W. W. Norton, 2004.
Gail B. Stewart. *Forensics.* Farmington Hills, MI: Thomson Gale, 2006.

Maya Royal Family
Clara Bezanilla. *A Pocket Dictionary of Aztec and Mayan Gods and Goddesses.* Los Angeles: J. Paul Getty Museum, 2010.
Vivien Bowers. *Crime Scene.* Toronto: Maple Tree Press, 2006.
Simon Boyce. *Royal Maya Massacre.* Washington: National Geographic, 2005. (DVD)
Dolores Gassos. *The Mayas.* Philadelphia: Chelsea House Publishers, 2006.
Nathanial Harris. *Ancient Maya: Archaeology Unlocks the Secrets to the Maya's Past.* Washington: National Geographic, 2008.
Fiona MacDonald. *The Aztec and Mayan Worlds.* New York: Rosen Publishing, 2009.

Napoleon Bonaparte
Georgia Bragg. *How They Croaked.* New York: Walker & Company, 2011.
Kimberley Burton Heuston. *Napoleon.* New York: Franklin Watts, 2010.
Adrian Hadland. *Who Was Napoleon?* London: Short Books, 2005.
Thierry Lentz. *Napoleon.* New York: Abrams, 2005.

The Man in the Iron Mask
Alexandre Dumas. *The Man in the Iron Mask.* New York: Marvel Publishing, 2008. (Graphic novel)
Lionel Fanthorpe. *The World's Most Mysterious Castles.* Toronto: Hounslow, 2005.
Hugh Ross Williamson. *Who Was the Man in the Iron Mask? And Other Historical Mysteries.* London: Penguin Classics, 2002.

King Rama VIII
Chris Cooper. *Forensic Science.* New York: Dorling Kindersley, 2008.
Ron Fridell. *Forensic Science.* Minneapolis: Lerner Publications, 2007.
Stacy Taus-Bolstad. *Thailand in Pictures.* Minneapolis: Lerner Publications, 2004.

Grand Duchess Anastasia

Hugh Brewster. *Anastasia's Album.* Toronto: Penguin Studio/Madison Press Books, 1996.

Hugh Brewster and Laurie Coulter. *To Be a Princess: The Fascinating Lives of Real Princesses.* Markham, ON: Scholastic Canada, 2001.

Kathleen Berton Murrell. *Russia.* Toronto: Stoddart, 1998.

Abraham Resnick. *Russia: A History to 1917.* Chicago: Children's Press, 1983.

King Tutankhamun

Diana Briscoe. *King Tut: Tales from the Tomb.* Mankato, MN: Capstone Press, 2003.

Susan Hughes. *Case Closed.* Toronto: Kids Can Press, 2010.

Michael Woods. *The Tomb of King Tutankhamen.* Minneapolis: Twenty-First Century Books, 2008.

Louis XVII

Kathryn Lasky. *Marie Antoinette: Princess of Versailles.* New York: Scholastic, 2000.

Nancy Lotz and Carlene Phillips. *Marie Antoinette and the Decline of French Monarchy.* Greensboro, NC: Morgan Reynolds, 2005.

Nancy Plain. *Louis XVI, Marie Antoinette, and the French Revolution.* New York: Benchmark Books, 2002.

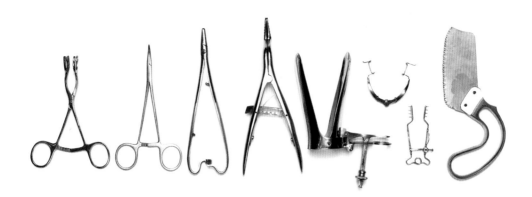

Image Credits

Front and back cover: map, © Marispro/Dreamstime.com; front cover: face and neck, © iStockphoto, Inc./David Marchal; tablet used throughout as on front and back cover, © Alexander Bryljaev/Dreamstime.com; four different angles of skull used throughout as on title page, © Noam Armonn/Dreamstime.com; test tubes used throughout as on Contents, © Viacheslav Krisanov/Dreamstime.com; blue glove used throughout as on Contents, © Brandon Alms/Dreamstime.com; Contents, 66: finger print kit, © Scol22/Dreamstime.com; red handprint used throughout as on page iv, © Igor Kovalchuk/Dreamstime.com; 7, © iStockphoto, Inc./Milan Lipowski; magnifying glass used throughout as on page 8, © Brandon Alms/Dreamstime.com; evidence bags used throughout as on page 9, 16, © Brandon Alms/Dreamstime.com; 10: x-ray of pelvis, © Deckard73/Dreamstime.com; tablet used throughout as on page 10, © Oblachko/Dreamstime.com; 12: the pool under excavation by the team of osteologists, © Andrew L. Demarest; evidence tag used throughout as on page 12, © Brandon Alms/Dreamstime.com; 13: Temple V, © Gudmund1/Dreamstime.com; 14: remains of Kan Maax, © Andrew L. Demarest; CAT scan roll used throughout as on page 14, © iStockphoto, Inc./oonal; beaker and DNA used throughout as on page 15, © iStockphoto, Inc./ewg3D; microscope used throughout as on page 16, © Les Cunliffe/Dreamstime.com; 19: jewelry, etc. buried with the massacre victims, © Andrew L. Demarest; mobile device used throughout as on page 20, © Profyart/Dreamstime.com; 20: forensic facial reconstruction sculpture, © B Christopher/Alamy; 23, © iStockphoto, Inc./Nicholas Monu; 25, © Photos.com; 26, © Danita Delimont/Alamy; 28, © Gillian Moore/Alamy; 30: ants, © Andrey Pavlov/Dreamstime.com; 30: cockroach, © Cammeraydave/Dreamstime.com; 30: flies, © Alain Lacroix/Dreamstime.com; computer used throughout as on page 33, © Leelaryonkul/Dreamstime.com; 33: bone saw, © Ekaterina Fribus/Dreamstime.com; 37: Napoleon, Library of Congress, Reproduction Number: LC-DIG-prokc-20099; monitor used throughout as on page 37, © Csuzda/Dreamstime.com; 38, Library of Congress, Reproduction Number: LC-DIG-ppmsca-09257; 41, © Curaga/Bigstock.com; 43, 44, © 2012 Jupiterimages Corporation; 46, © iStockphoto, Inc./horstklinker; mobile phone used throughout as on 48, © Alexander Bryljaev/Dreamstime.com; 48, © Photos.com; 51 left, Alfredo Dagli Orti/The Art Archive at Art Resource, NY; 51 right, © iStockphoto, Inc./pictore; 53, © Ulia Zotanina/Dreamstime.com; 55: fabric, © Alexander Shevchenko/Dreamstime.com; 55: letters, © Milan Kopcok/Dreamstime.com; 56, Library of Congress, Reproduction Number: LC-DIG-ppmsca-07185; 61, © Edward Bartel/ Dreamstime.com; 63, © Puwanai Ponchai/Dreamstime.com; 65, Bureau of the Royal Household, Kingdom of Thailand; 68, © Aleksandar Kosev/Dreamstime.com; 71, © AP Photo; 73, © Olira/Dreamstime.com; 75, AP Photo; 79, © Calyx22/Dreamstime.com; 81, Library of Congress, Reproduction Number: LC-DIG-hec-04746; 82, © Dmitry Gorelov/Dreamstime.com; 84, Beinecke Rare Book and Manuscript Library, Yale University; 86, Library of Congress, Reproduction Number: LC-DIG-ggbain-38336; 89, Library of Congress, Reproduction Number: LC-DIG-ggbain-17558; 92, © Bettmann/CORBIS; 95, © Michaela Stejskalova/Dreamstime.com; 98, © HO Images/Alamy; 101, © thefinalmiracle/Bigstock.com; 103, © iStockphoto, Inc./The Power of Forever Photography; 105, © Prehor/Dreamstime.com; 107, © iStockphoto, Inc./Luke Daniek; 109, © David Cole/Alamy; 111, © Vesna Njagulj/Dreamstime.com; 113, © iStockphoto, Inc./a-r-t-i-s-t; 115, © Danita Delimont/Alamy; 117, © Danita Delimont/Alamy; 119, © iStockphoto, Inc./The Power of Forever Photography; 121, © Picstudio/Dreamstime.com; 123, © kj-pargeter/Bigstock.com; 125, courtesy Jean DAVID; 127, Gianni Dagli Orti/The Art Archive at Art Resource, NY; 128, © Ivy Close Images/Alamy; 131, © 2012 Jupiterimages Corporation; 132, © Perseomedusa/Dreamstime.com; 135, © Olga Shkoda/Dreamstime.com; 137, © Lculig/Dreamstime.com; 138, © 4designersart/Dreamstime.com; 140, © Kingjon/ Dreamstime.com; 143 left, © 2012 Jupiterimages Corporation; 143 right, Library of Congress, Reproduction Number: LC-USZ62-75036; 145, © Kheng Ho Toh/Dreamstime.com; 152, © Ekaterina Fribus/Dreamstime.com

Index

5/14